Visual Design Concepts
for Mobile Games

Visual Design Concepts for Mobile Games

by

Christopher Carman

CRC Press
Taylor & Francis Group
Boca Raton London New York

CRC Press is an imprint of the
Taylor & Francis Group, an **informa** business
A FOCAL PRESS BOOK

CRC Press
Taylor & Francis Group
6000 Broken Sound Parkway NW, Suite 300
Boca Raton, FL 33487-2742

© 2018 by Taylor & Francis Group, LLC
CRC Press is an imprint of Taylor & Francis Group, an Informa business

No claim to original U.S. Government works

Printed on acid-free paper

International Standard Book Number-13: 978-1-1388-0692-4 (Paperback)
International Standard Book Number-13: 978-0-8153-6651-5 (Hardback)

Library of Congress Cataloging-in-Publication Data

Names: Carman, Christopher, author.
Title: Visual design concepts for mobile games / Christopher Carman.
Description: Boca Raton : Taylor & Francis, a CRC title, part of the Taylor & Francis imprint, a member of the Taylor & Francis Group, the academic division of T&F Informa, plc, [2018]
Identifiers: LCCN 2017034803| ISBN 9780815366515 (hardback : alk. paper) | ISBN 9781138806924 (pbk. : alk. paper)
Subjects: LCSH: Visual programming (Computer science) | Computer graphics. | Video games--Design.
Classification: LCC QA76.65 .C37 2018 | DDC 006.6--dc23
LC record available at https://lccn.loc.gov/2017034803

Visit the Taylor & Francis Web site at
http://www.taylorandfrancis.com

and the CRC Press Web site at
http://www.crcpress.com

Contents

Preface

A quick note on tools before we get started:

The tools covered within this text combine both traditional (pencils, pens, etc.) and digital (Adobe Photoshop CS4 and up) drawing hardware, including Wacom products such as the Intuos graphics tablet and/or Cintiq interactive displays. This text assumes that the reader has a beginner to intermediate level of drawing and painting ability. In addition, a basic working knowledge of Photoshop's interface and tool sets is highly encouraged and can be found at Adobe's website (https://helpx.adobe.com/photoshop/tutorials.html).

Acknowledgments

Thanks to Zynga, Rovio, Blowfish Studios, BYXB, and all the talented participating artists who allowed their work to be reproduced within:

Ciaee Ching:
http://ciaee.net/

Alexandra DePasse:
http://alexandradepasse.com/

Siena Han:
https://www.sienahan.com/

Myisha Haynes:
http://myishaart.tumblr.com/

Mark Henriksen:
https://www.artstation.com/markhenriksen

Florencia Kristiani:
https://www.artstation.com/florenciakristiani

Juan Lopez:
https://www.behance.net/jjlopez

John Nevarez:
https://johnnevarez.carbonmade.com/

Brandon Pike:
http://brandonpikeportfolio.blogspot.com

Mark Oliver:
http://www.olly.net/

Leonardo Romano:
http://www.leonardoromano.com/

Yu Chin (Sunny) Tien:
https://sunnytienart.carbonmade.com/

Tony Trujillo:
http://www.tonytrujilloart.com

Kim Truong:
http://ktruongart.tumblr.com/

Jung Hyun (Hyoni) Yim:
https://www.hyoniyim.com/

Special thanks to my wife Jetangline Villaflor, whose feedback and design support were invaluable, and to Sean Connelly and Focal Press for the opportunity to produce this text.

About the Author

Christopher Carman has operated in the role of Art Director and Designer in the web, mobile, and console games industry for the past decade with a client list that includes Electronic Arts, Zynga, MTV Games, and Adobe. He currently serves as the Associate Director of Visual Development at the Academy of Art University in San Francisco, California.

http://chriscarmanart.com/

Chapter 1

Isometric Perspective

CHAPTER OBJECTIVES

In this first chapter, we will examine the origins of "social" (mobile/web) games and establish what makes them different from traditional console and PC games. We'll begin by examining the isometric perspective and why historically it's been effective for mobile and PC game development. In addition, we will walk through the various priorities to consider when designing within an isometric environment by completing the assignment at the end of this chapter (Assignment 1.1).

KEY LEARNING OUTCOMES

- Identify and define the term "social" game.
- Understand the basic priorities of isometric perspective.

EXERCISE/ASSIGNMENT

- Exercise 1.1: Play Some Games!
- Assignment 1.1: "The Saloon" (3–4) hours

What Is (and Isn't) This Book about?

Let's kick things off by talking about what this book is and what it is not. This book is geared toward both students and professionals who are looking to enter the mobile (tablet/smartphone) and PC (personal computer) industry as concept artists (for both 2D and 3D production pipelines) or 2D production artists (game-ready assets). This book is not specifically focused on game design or game development and is also not a 3D modeling or animation guide.

However, certain aspects of game design, game development, and 3D modeling and animation will impact the visual development and art creation process. So, at points throughout, we will explore topics such as game engine performance and game mechanics, though at a very high-level, bird's-eye vantage point and only as they pertain to the visual development of the various assignments throughout this book.

"Adventureland." (From Zynga, copyright 2009–2017. With permission.)

Isometric Game Board Template

Through the completion of exercises and assignments contained within each chapter, readers will be guided through the visual development process and execution of a variety of concepts and assets (final game art). This will include categories such as *characters, props*, and *backgrounds* within an *isometric* design template. The categories themselves will relate more to their function within a *very* simple game design template than their completed visual representation (e.g., the "big buildable" category could be anything from a town square to a fire-breathing dragon, as long as it fits within the bare-bones parameters of the asset type's functionality). The concept, theme, and style of these assets, as well as the world they inhabit, will be completely up to the artist.

In addition to the isometric view, there are several other game screen perspectives that are commonly used in web and mobile games such as:

Side Scroll:

"Tiny Thief." (From Rovio, copyright 2009–2017. With permission.)

Top Down:

"Stampede Run." (From Zynga, copyright 2009–2017. With permission.)

However, for the visual development purposes of this book, we will be focusing the majority of our attention on the standard isometric environment, which we'll explore further in this chapter.

With this in mind, we will be examining and developing additional assets outside of the isometric environment, including marketing art (box art, posters, etc.), game loading screens, simple user interface (UI) elements, and a supplemental *side-scroll concept* in Chapters 12–14 of this book.

What Exactly Is a "Social" Game?

A common designation given to the type of game that this book will explore is "social" game. So, what is a "social game" and what makes it different from a traditional console (Xbox, PlayStation, etc.) or PC (World of Warcraft, Civilization, etc.) game?

Before we get into what specifically "social games" are, let's step back a bit and establish what a *video game* is in the broadest sense. Simply put, games are where engineering, visual arts, and interactive design merge to create an experience/

product. An "allspice" of media, if you will. The term "social" games was coined to describe game design mechanics that integrate viral channels native to social media platforms such as Facebook into games for propagation and player acquisition purposes. The "Lonely Animal" feature of "FarmVille" is an example of an early social game success.

"FarmVille." (From Zynga, copyright 2009–2017. With permission.)

However, when we use the term "social games" anywhere within this text, it's in reference to any of the current market of mobile and web-based games with a multiple player function—whether synchronous ("World of Warcraft") or asynchronous ("Connect Four"), these games are inherently "social."

As social networking sites such as Facebook and Myspace functioned as the early platform for these games, the more recent "Blue Ocean" (area with the most opportunity for growth) is considered to be mobile and tablet gaming (made up primarily of the Apple and Android app stores). However, the fractured nature of the mobile market as of this writing has made it difficult for one company to establish dominance and utilize resources such as marketing and advertising dollars to drive user acquisition.

Much like any digital market, the mobile space is ripe for disruption and commonly sees "indie" games (produced by smaller game development teams) race to the top of the download charts. "Flappy Birds," by lone developer Dong Nguyen, is an excellent example of this disruption.

While the hits-driven nature of the video game industries can pose challenges for a large established game developer to build a predictable business around, particularly with the web/mobile sector due to the lower barrier to entry, the prospect of a single developer uprooting the big players of the industry is both exciting and a unique opportunity that is not currently present in most other entertainment sectors.

Note: That from the perspective of this book, the visual development process from concept art to completed assets between web and mobile in general will be approached as one and the same. Any differing aspects that impact the visual development process for either platform will be noted.

The Evolution of Social Game Art

Early social games such as "Mafia Wars" and other text-based RPGs (role playing games) were much simpler to build from both game design and art creation perspectives when compared to the titles being published by traditional console game developers.

"Mafia Wars." (From Zynga, copyright 2009–2017. With permission.)

Basic leader boards and puzzle games were the initial offerings on social networking platforms (Facebook, Myspace, Friendster). From a visual development and asset creation perspective, these games required little in the way of complex animation (which tends to be very processor intensive) and consisted primarily of static imagery.

As these social platforms opened up for third-party game development, there was a rapid land grab and quick movers were able carve out their slice of the player bases. This had an immediate impact on game design and art creation as the combination of lightning fast production cycles, the platforms' limited technology to support games, and the simple fact that most of the early players were by no means "gamers" in the traditional sense meant that their expectations of complex game mechanics and graphics were greatly reduced. While the games were fun and engaging, these factors contributed to a lack of sophistication in the overall game experience of these early offerings, at least when compared to the larger budgeted and mature development environments of console gaming.

The Isometric Explosion

When the original "FarmVille" launched on the Facebook platform in July 2009, it pushed the concept of social games into the mainstream lexicon. Through the viral channels mentioned previously, "FarmVille" was able to amass more than 30 million players a day within just a few months of launching, a number previously unheard of in any form of gaming. The virality of the game ushered in a gold-rush mentality throughout the game industry, where numerous isometric games that utilized the simple yet effective mechanics of *plow, plant, harvest, repeat* appeared on the Facebook platform.

"FarmVille." (From Zynga, copyright 2009–2017. With permission.)

Due to the success of "FarmVille" and games similar to it, the Facebook platform became saturated with an increasing number of gaming options. In addition, the player base was maturing at a rapid rate and beginning to demand a more sophisticated (and less buggy) product. As a result, the time and budgets spent developing games

"FarmVille." (From Zynga, copyright 2009–2017. With permission.)

"CastleVille." (From Zynga, copyright
2009–2017. With permission.)

"CastleVille." (From Zynga, copyright
2009–2017. With permission.)

increased dramatically. Development cycles began to increase from several months to, in some cases, several years. The results of this increased emphasis on the cohesiveness and polish of the design and art can be seen in "CastleVille" and "FarmVille" imagery to the left and below.

The adoption of 3D engines such as Unity as well as the recent versions of Flash Player in web and mobile game development has allowed for increasing complex animation, lighting, and texture in game assets. An example of this is the evolution of the art from the original "FarmVille" to its sequel, "FarmVille 2."

Advancements in the Flash engine used for both has allowed for real-time 3D graphics in "FarmVille 2." But in addition to the technological advancements, preproduction time was spent establishing a much more rendered and realistic "painterly" approach the art style that manages to build upon the playful and appealing aesthetic of its 2D, vector art driven, predecessor.

Note that we'll be exploring vector tools in Chapter 2.

"FarmVille Cow." (From Zynga, copyright
2009–2017. With permission.)

"FarmVille 2 Cow." (From Zynga, copyright
2009–2017. With permission.)

"FarmVille" Game Board Screen

"FarmVille." (From Zynga, copyright 2009–2017. With permission.)

"FarmVille 2" Game Board Screen

"FarmVille 2." (From Zynga, copyright 2009–2017. With permission.)

What's This Isometric Perspective We Keep Hearing about?

We've been referring to the isometric explosion in games, but what specifically is the isometric perspective? What are the strengths and weaknesses of designing within it? Well, drawing and designing within the isometric view are akin to drawing objects in an environment lacking a visible horizon as well as vanishing points and is based on the diamond-shaped grid seen in the following:

This has been historically a very effective method of creating a scene in gaming and goes all the way back to the earliest days of game development. As with multiple objects rendered in this same method, the modular nature of the isometric perspective allows for freedom of movement throughout the grid.

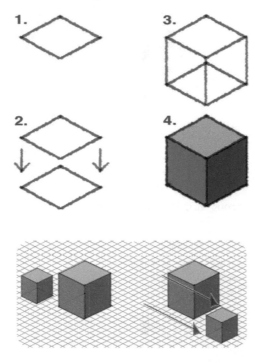

Due to the lack of horizon line and vanishing points, adjusting objects due to perspective changes (diminution, vanishing points, etc.) is not a concern. As we can see in the image on the next page, the smaller cube can be moved freely around the game board—its relationship to the larger cube remains intact, and the illusion of depth is preserved. This modular nature is ideal for games, as an artist can create a multitude of assets and move them freely throughout a gameboard without having to worry about pesky perspective issues.

Due to the isometric perspective being, as we mentioned earlier, essentially a perspectiveless environment (no vanishing points or horizon line), the ability to create drama and depth through traditional perspective arrangements is not as readily available to us. At a quick glance, an artist might assume that the isometric perspective's is a rigid and sterile design environ-

ment due to its gridded arrangement; however looking closer an isometric perspective can elicit a variety of unique emotions including:

- Simplicity

- Calm

- Stability

- Birds-eye view/"god view"—gives the viewer a dominant vantage

- Order—gridded structure

- Retro/nostalgic—reminds us of the earliest video games

When designing an image with these unique characteristics in mind, an artist can use the isometric perspective

Mark Oliver "Hastings Poster"

to communicate a variety of complex emotions.

A scene such as that in the illustration to the right could sound fairly intense when described on paper: "a massive, ten-tacled creature emerges from the ocean to attack a coastal community." However, when presented in isometric perspective (coupled with a warm color palette and rounded shape design of the characters), the scene has a peaceful, organized, and calming appearance.

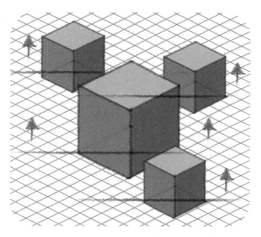

Stacking

Another simple, yet important, concept to keep in mind when seeking to achieve the illusion of depth in an isometric design is the concept of "stacking," where whichever object is lowest on the game board is considered closest to us (or in front). The higher the object is, the further away. This is important, as we mentioned earlier we do not have the traditional means of creating depth (diminution, vanishing points, etc.) at our disposal.

EXERCISE 1.1   PLAY SOME GAMES!

Play at least one of each of the following types of games:

- Isometric

- Side-scroll

- Additional

Take notes on design aesthetics, as well what you think is working visually and what is not. Focus on the visual design of the game (e.g., "I found the overall color scheme of the game to be somewhat confusing and over saturated") and *not* specific game play elements (e.g., "I found it confusing when player x couldn't move object y.")

ASSIGNMENT 1.1   "THE SALOON" (3–4) HOURS

Isometric Grid

Tools

Adobe Photoshop or Traditional tools (pen, pencils, paper, etc.)

Description

This first assignment will give us a chance to establish comfort with the isometric environment and act as a primer prior to beginning the isometric game board project we will begin in Chapter 3.

Using the isomeric template provided, sketch out an exterior "saloon" scene in isometric view that includes:

Isometric Template

- Two characters

- One saloon structure

- One vehicle

- Two small props (e.g., signs, newspaper stand, etc.).

For the setting/aesthetic of this "saloon," there are three options:

- Futuristic Tokyo (e.g., *Blade Runner, Akira*)

- Medieval Europe (e.g., *The Hunchback of Notre Dame, The Sword in the Stone*)

- Wild West (e.g., *Rango, Home on the Range, Unforgiven*)

(Continued)

ASSIGNMENT 1.1 (CONTINUED)   "THE SALOON" (3–4) HOURS

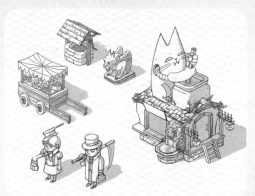

Sienna Han "Isometric Saloon"

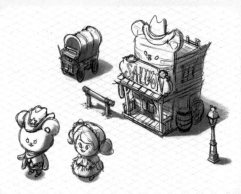

Yu-Chin Tien "Isometric Saloon"

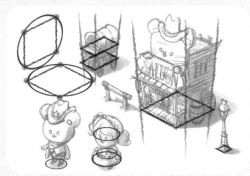

For whichever time period/theme you select, make sure that the design of the generic categories is convincing with referenced costumes, architecture, design aesthetics, materials, and so on. For example, in a "Wild West" saloon scene, "vehicles" would be steam powered or horse drawn, and "smaller props" could consist of tombstones, hitching posts, and so on. Remember—no interiors! Your scene must be an exterior of a saloon.

Isometric Drawing Tips

- Ellipses (red) such as cast shadows, eye lines, and barrels need to be properly pitched to create the convincing isometric perspective. To create ellipses in the isometric perspective, use the box (purple) as a reference tool.
- "Loosen" up your verticals (green). Take note of the building and wagon's verticals, as they are subtly hinting at a vanishing point below, which helps to provide some playfulness and scale to an otherwise stiff perspective format.

Conclusion

In this chapter, we covered the origins of "social" games, what makes them unique, and what particular factors informed their visual arts evolution. We were also introduced to working within an isometric environment and an examination of why this format has been historically a good fit for mobile and PC games. Finally, we sketched out our own isometric environment based around a "saloon" (Wild West/future Tokyo/medieval Europe) design assignment.

Quiz

1.1   An isometric perspective can elicit a variety of unique emotional responses, including nostalgia and calm. T/F

1.2   Basic leader boards and puzzle games were typical of early social games. T/F

1.3   Smaller development teams never succeed in the mobile games sector. T/F

1.4   An isometric perspective includes a visible horizon line. T/F

1.5   Stacking can achieve the illusion of depth in an isometric environment. T/F

Chapter 2

Vector Tools

CHAPTER OBJECTIVES

In this chapter, we will explore the vector art toolset available in Adobe Photoshop while comparing the strengths and weaknesses of *bitmap* versus *vector* image formats. We will also familiarize ourselves with the vector tools native to Adobe Photoshop, utilizing them to complete the exercise and assignment.

KEY LEARNING OUTCOMES

- Understand the vector tools native to Adobe Photoshop.
- Complete a vector apple exercise.
- Complete vector saloon assets.

EXERCISE/ASSIGNMENT

- Exercise 2.1: Vector Apple (1) hour
- Assignment 2.1: Vector "Saloon" Assets (3–4) hours

Bitmaps

When embarking on the visual development process for any mobile or PC game, it is important to understand the differences between the two major 2D graphic image types: *bitmap* and *vector*. This is an important concept to grasp, as it's bound to come up within a game art pipeline. Bitmap images (or raster images) are, simply put, images made up of pixels, which appear as tiny dots of color onscreen. When these pixels (or dots) are combined, they form an image. Most computer monitors display approximately 70 to 100 pixels per inch—the actual number depends on your monitor and screen settings. The following image illustrates the concept of a pixel grid.

If you were to count the number of pixels in this image, you would find there are 58 (width) × 58 (height). The higher an image's pixel count, the sharper the image will appear. As a result bitmap images are what's known as *resolution dependent*. The resolution of an image results from the number of pixels and is represented the form of "dpi" (dots per inch) or "ppi" (pixels per inch). As bitmap images are resolution dependent, it can be difficult to increase their size without some degradation in image quality, usually a blurring of the original image.

To reduce the size of a bitmap image, your software must "throw away" pixels. To increase the size of a bitmap image, your software has to create new pixels, which it does by estimating the color values of the new pixels based on surrounding pixels. This process is called *interpolation*. An important note to make is the difference between *scaling* an image and *resizing* an image. *Scaling* refers only to zooming in and out on a particular image and does *not* affect the image permanently. *Resizing*, however, (such as through the Photoshop Image > Image Size commands) will impact the image quality—particularly if you are increasing the size of your image (adding pixels). The following are the most common types of bitmap file formats and the programs that generate and handle them. Those in bold are program/file types that are most commonly used in a game development pipeline for final assets (in-game art), whereas others such as PSD and TIFF are reserved for the larger source art files that ultimately generate the final in-game images.

Common bitmap formats:

- BMP

- GIF

- **JPEG (JPG)**

- **PNG**

- PCX

- TIFF

- PSD (Adobe Photoshop)

Programs to create and edit bitmaps:

- **Adobe Photoshop**

- Corel Photo-Paint

- Corel Paint Shop Pro

- Microsoft Paint

Vectors

While not as commonly used as bitmaps, vectors hold several distinct advantages over the bitmap format in that they are made up of individual scalable objects as opposed to a collection of pixels. Thus, they never degrade in quality as you resize them.

Vector (left) versus Bitmap (right)

This ability to scale is incredibly valuable for not only game development but all design fields, as it means images created using vector objects are *resolution independent*. Thus, we can increase and decrease the size of vector images, to any degree, and the image will remain crisp and sharp, both on screen and in print. Fonts are an additional type of vector object. This scalability afforded by vectors means that, for instance, a publisher would not have to deal with image degradation if they were to resize an illustration from a video game box cover for use as a billboard image advertisement. Had the publisher's illustration been created

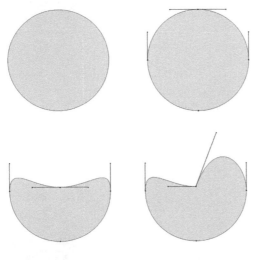

using bitmaps, it would likely need significant repainting for it to be a high enough resolution for that large of a presentation. However, if the original box art was completed using vector objects, no additional work would be required because vectors are what? That's right, *resolution independent*.

The scalable objects that vectors consist of are generated by the placement of points. These objects can consist of lines, curves, and primitive shapes that are generated through complex math. This complex math is what lets vector objects scale without any loss in image quality. An added bonus is that depending on the complexity of the vector image, it can be a much smaller file size than a bitmap image, which makes it "lightweight" and processor friendly (however, this diminishes as the number of vector points that make up the various objects increases).

While vectors have many advantages, the primary disadvantage when utilizing these tools is that they do not lend well to rendering photo-realistic or painterly imagery—a result of being made up of shapes/objects. This can be a wall for many painters/illustrators, as it forces an artist to be very methodical and economical with elements such as detail when executing a design.

That being said, with patience and planning, you can still achieve some fairly complex imagery (such as the following examples).

Vector Tools

Let's talk a bit about the vector tools available in Adobe Photoshop. If you're familiar with the vector tools in Adobe Illustrator, then you're in luck because the Photoshop vector toolset is for all intents and purposes a simplified version of that program's tools. Adobe Illustrator does offer a far more robust set of vector features and options; however, with the workflow many traditional illustrators and concept artists employ (this author included), there's typically a level of comfort working within the Adobe Photoshop environment. The ability to set up bitmap sketches/color studies and proceed right into the construction of vector objects for tasks such as final game assets within the same source file, without having to navigate between multiple programs, can be very advantageous to

The Business End "Nice Marmot" (Album Cover)

a game artist's workflow. In addition, the tools offered exclusively within Illustrator (primarily the vector gradient tools) tend to be more processor heavy, from a game engine standpoint, to render. This specifically can be prohibitive for game development as the limitations of individual players' hardware mean all aspects of production, from art to code, need to be as lightweight as possible, particularly in the mobile sector, where there are strict ceilings on file sizes. As a result, working with the stripped-down vector tools Adobe Photoshop offers can be a good way for an artist to avoid the temptation of those expensive performance-draining features such as said gradients. In this chapter, we will cover the simplified vector tools in Photoshop; however, if for some reason an artist is more comfortable or has prior experience with Adobe Illustrator's vector tools, then I encourage you to execute any vector-based assignments and exercises in that program. In the end, whether an object is created in Photoshop, Illustrator, Toon Boom, or another similar program, it's still a vector object and carries all the advantages, and disadvantages, previously described.

Shape Tools in Adobe Photoshop

So, let's get started exploring these vector tools we've been hearing about.

Looking at the following image, we can see that Photoshop's various shape tools are all nested together in the Tools panel. By default, the Rectangle tool is the shape tool that's visible, but if you click on the tool's icon and hold your mouse button down, a fly-out menu will appear, listing the additional shape tools that are available, including a "Rounded Rectangle Tool," an "Ellipse Tool," and so on. We'll start with the Ellipse tool from the list, but everything we discuss related to this tool applies to all of the shape tools, not just the Ellipse tool.

Drawing Modes

Once you've chosen a shape tool, you will need to select which type of object—shape, path, or pixels—you would like to utilize, which you can do using the Drawing Mode options located on the left side of the options bar (circled in green).

When creating any vector art, you'll want to select the "Shape" mode, as "*Path*" mode is what's called a *nondisplay object* and is used for the creation of selections and clipping masks, while the "Pixel" mode is used to create the pixel-based layers that are resolution dependent and therefore do not provide the advantages—such as the scalability—of working with vectors.

Drawing Shape Layers (Vector Shapes)

To draw vector shapes, first select the Pen tool from your toolbar then make sure the Shape Layers option is selected in the options bar:

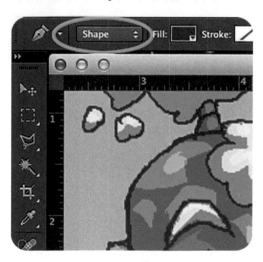

Let's take a quick look in a layer's panel, where we see that currently the document is made up of nothing more than a single layer—the background layer—which is by default filled with solid white:

You can choose a color for your vector shape by clicking on the Fill color swatch on the options bar:

Once you've selected the Pen tool, double check that it is set it to "Shape," select a color, then you're free to start creating vector art.

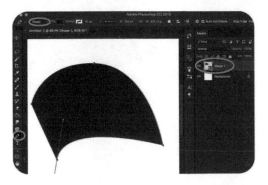

Chapter 3

Isometric Game Board Project Introduction

CHAPTER OBJECTIVES

In this chapter, we will look at the priorities associated with the commencing of any creative project, including web and mobile video games. We will look at the initial stages of reference gathering, assembling a vision board, and the creation of exploration sketches that will be the first step in the completion of your personalized "isometric game board."

KEY LEARNING OUTCOMES

- Define the approach to the early stages of visual development for a web/mobile game.
- Collect and organize imagery for both the functional (props, costumes) and the inspirational (mood, aesthetic, etc.) reference categories.
- Generate initial exploration sketches for a personalized "isometric game board."

EXERCISE/ASSIGNMENT

- Exercise 3.1: Vision Board
- Assignment 3.1: Initial Exploration Sketches (3–4) hours

Introduction to the "Isometric Game Board" Project

In this chapter's exercise and assignment, you will begin your personalized "isometric game board," the creation of which will continue throughout the remaining chapters of this book. This completed "isometric game board" will take the form of game-ready isometric environment that will consist of multiple asset types, including *characters, props,* and a *finished background game board.* The project's narrative, gameplay, setting, and overall visual aesthetic are entirely up to the artist/reader, as the project's parameters have been designed in a way to accommodate all manner of themes ranging from a medieval combat setting:

"Dawn of Titans." (From Zynga, copyright 2009–2017. With permission.)

To a cute and whimsical resource management:

"CastleVille." (From Zynga, copyright 2009–2017. With permission.)

Or even something as offbeat as a surrealist landscape:

Salvador Dali "The Temptation of St. Anthony" (1946). (Courtesy of Wikipedia, Metamorphosis of Narcissus, https://en.wikipedia.org/wiki/Metamorphosis_of_Narcissus, last modified on July 12, 2017.)

There will be plenty of opportunities for the artist to have fun and express himself or herself within this project. A few words of advice: *keep it simple.* Do not attempt to write a novel or design a fully fleshed-out game design document (multiple levels, currency, economy, etc.). If you can't sum up your project's theme in one sentence, then it is overly complicated. "A puzzle solving/mystery game set at the turn of the nineteenth century in Victorian England" is more than enough to get started with reference gathering, vision board, and initial exploration sketches.

Note: That the materials and processes contained in this book from this point forward will reflect the creation of the assets described earlier but as a reader, you will be able to follow along without opting into the project if you so choose.

Reference

The first step of a project of any type (game, film, etc.) or scale (game level, film scene, etc.) is reviewing the associated documentation. This documentation can take several forms depending on the particular medium. For instance, in the film industry, that documentation is typically the *script*, whereas in the video game industry, it often takes the form of a *game design document*. This will act as your guide as you establish the parameters for your reference gathering (and the overall project in general). For the purposes of this chapter and the project mentioned previously, selecting a story/theme that interests you visually and keeps you engaged for the remainder of the exercises and assignments should be enough to start the reference gathering process.

When gathering references via books, magazines, trips to museums, or the ever-convenient Internet, it's important to thoroughly saturate yourself with imagery. For example, if you're kicking off visual development for a first-person shooter video game set during World War II ala-"Call of Duty," you're going to want to dive headfirst into images and materials from the period such as documentary footage, films set during the time period ("Saving Private Ryan," "Captain America: The First Avenger," etc.), and such as propaganda posters from the period. As you will be collecting a large number of images, it's advantageous to organize them into two categories: *functional* and *inspirational*.

Photo of World War II Soldiers. (Courtesy of Wikipedia, Battle of Okinawa, HYPERLINK https://en.wikipedia.org/wiki/Battle_of_ Okinawa#/media/File:Ww2_158.jpg, last modified on November 25, 2017.)

Functional

The functional category covers everything specific to a particular subject. Using the World War II setting as an example, this would include everything from the imagery for the types weapons used to location photos where combat took place to the model/make of tanks present. These reference images will become increasingly important as you move toward completed assets, as they will infuse your designs with a sense of authenticity.

Schlaikier "Propaganda Poster." (Courtesy of Wikipedia, American propaganda during World War II, https://en.wikipedia.org/wiki/American_propaganda_during_World_War_II#/media/File:In_the_face_of_obstacles_-_Courage_poster.jpg, last modified on November 29, 2017.)

Inspirational

The inspirational category can include anything from specific artists or projects that you're initially inspired by to imagery that may have little to do with the subject of the piece and more to do with a specific color palette, texture/pattern, or treatment of line that you feel may be appropriate for the project. Examples could include the delicate line work of Windsor McCay's *Little Nemo in Slumberland* or the muted/rusted color palette used in the video game "Machinarium" by Amanita Design.

Keep in mind there's no such thing as too much reference material, and don't worry about editing down the number of images you've gathered. But do look to organize your imagery in manner so that they can be easily located as needed. Individual folders for guns, vehicles, architecture, color palettes, and so on are recommended.

By exposing yourself to the imagery and information that relates to your subject, you will be absorbing key elements (such as *basic shape design*, *materials*, and *color palette*) as you go. Then when you are approaching the next stage of visual development—the initial exploration sketches—you will be able to quickly generate your rough sketches, ideally without having to refer back to your reference images continuously (which can impede your ability to rapidly sketch out ideas). These initial sketches, by nature, are meant to be loose, covering broad strokes more than specific details. Later, when you start to zero in on your visual target for individual assets, these specific functional references will become more important, as they will give your designs added credibility.

Note: That an alternative and more dynamic approach to reference gathering combines your initial sketches with your reference gathering process. Small sketches and notes made as you compile imagery allow you to immediately generate ideas based on your reference material. This is encouraged as long as you're able to keep moving through the imagery and can resist the urge to linger on one particular drawing or subject for too long.

Vision Board

Once you've gathered a robust assortment of reference images and organized them to cover both the *functional* and the *inspirational* aspects of your project, you're ready to move to the next stage of your project—assembling the vision board. In essence, your vision board should sum up in one sheet or board the visual aesthetic you're looking to achieve with any given project. As a result, the images you use will likely be weighted more to the *inspirational* side of your reference gathering. This board is by no means set in stone; it is merely a jumping off point for yourself and an easy (and quick) way to communicate to someone else (be it a producer, an art director, or a casual viewer) what you're hoping to visually achieve with a project.

Vision Board Template

With the selected reference imagery, look to identify:

- *Color scheme*—Is there a through line with the color palettes of your various reference images? A warm nostalgic palette? Cool and mysterious? Is it an analogous color palette? Triadic?

- *Shape design*—Are your reference images dominated by friendly rounded shapes? Aggressive angular?

- *Graphic versus volumetric design*—We'll get into this more in the character design chapters.

- *Texture/pattern*—Are there any particular patterns or textures that repeat throughout the references that are unique to your theme/aesthetic?

Using your previously gathered references, you will assemble a vision board of your own as an initial visual kickoff in this chapter's exercise (7 to 12 images should be plenty for your vision board). Your goal should be to assemble a vision board that will help to sum up for yourself and quickly communicate to others what the tone, look, and feel of your project will be.

Initial Explorations

Once you have compiled a vision board that clearly conveys the visual aesthetic of your new project, the next step of the production pipeline will be your "initial explorations"—quick sketches of several asset types that fit into your project's theme and world. This assignment will be very similar to the earlier "saloon" assignment from Chapter 1 in that you will be looking to quickly sketch out multiple designs for asset types that are all part of the same cohesive scene/setting. Therefore, the various assets should be designed convincingly through appropriate costumes, materials, and so on.

Beginning the initial exploration sketches in an isometric perspective is not always ideal, as focusing on *design* while also trying to draw accurately in such a challenging perspective can be tricky. A simple solution is to break the initial sketches into two rounds by approaching the design-heavy first round independent from the isometric environment and then focusing on translating those early designs to the isometric perspective for the second round.

Kim Truong "Initial Exploration Sketches"

In the following example, the artist began by sketching out concepts free of the isometric environment in a more standard "straight-on" perspective. Keep in mind that polish at this point is not a priority; however, clarity is.

With this first batch of sketches, the artist then proceeded to translate those designs to the isometric format. A benefit of the additional round is that the artist is able to continue to refine the designs during the second round of isometric perspective sketches.

In addition, a first round of sketches will by no means be wasted, as we'll be able to utilize these (nonisometric) sketches later in the project for assets such as marketing materials and game icons.

Kim Truong "Initial Exploration Sketches"

EXERCISE 3.1   VISION BOARD

Description

For this exercise, you will be tasked with deciding on a theme/story to base your assets on and then assembling a vision board using the reference material that you gathered in preparation for your "isometric game board." About 7 to 12 images from your inspirational reference folder should suffice. Take a look at the examples provided in this chapter for further inspiration.

Priorities include:

- Clear and cohesive visual aesthetic and theme

- Simple story/theme—Taking an existing well-known property such as a fairy tale and moving it to a different setting and/or time period can make for some exciting possibilities, for example, Peter Pan in feudal Japan or maybe Tarzan in a posta-pocalyptic setting

VISION BOARD
YOUR PROJECTS NAME:

Vision Board Template

Purpose

Using your gathered reference, compile a vision board that sums up the visual aesthetic you're looking to achieve with your "isometric game board."

Materials

Adobe Photoshop

ASSIGNMENT 3.1   INITIAL EXPLORATION SKETCHES (3–4) HOURS

Myisha Haynes "Initial Exploration Sketches"

Description

In this assignment, we will be completing the initial exploration sketches for the isometric game board project. To complete this assignment, you will need to have decided on a theme/story for your project, compiled appropriate reference images, and completed a vision board. The following images are representative of the minimum level of detail and finish for your assets. One clear light source and a clear understanding of designing in an isometric environment are required.

Using the isomeric template provided in Chapter 1, sketch:

- Two characters (one hero and one sidekick or villain)

- One large element (e.g., building, weapon, vehicle)

- Four smaller props (e.g., signs, newspaper stand)

Priorities should be:

- Convincing isometric perspective

- Shadow layer (based on a single light source)

- Cohesive design elements (shape, material, etc.)

Alexandra DePasse "Initial Exploration Sketches"

(Continued)

ASSIGNMENT 3.1 (CONTINUED)   INITIAL EXPLORATION SKETCHES (3–4) HOURS

Purpose

The purpose of this exercise is to begin the initial stages of designing your personalized "isometric game board."

Materials

Adobe Photoshop

Conclusion

In this chapter, we established the importance of thorough and organized reference gathering. By using our assembled reference images, we were able to complete a vision board to help communicate the visual aesthetic we're looking to achieve with our project. Finally, we have begun the initial exploration sketches for our personalized "isometric game board."

Quiz

3.1 Inspirational reference images are those that authenticate and provide credibility for a particular subject. T/F

3.2 Reference images should be organized in two categories: functional and inspirational. T/F

3.3 Initial explorations are quick concepts that convey the visual aesthetic of a project. T/F

Chapter 4

2D: The Pitch

CHAPTER OBJECTIVES

In this chapter, we will take a high-level overview of a typical 2D game development pipeline as well examine what makes for an effective product pitch. We will also be introduced to the thumbnails process and how it fits into a mobile and web game production.

KEY LEARNING OUTCOMES

- Gain a high-level understanding of the workings of a standard 2D game asset pipeline.
- Understand the thumbnails process of a game production pipeline.
- Complete the "thumbnails" stage of the final project.

ASSIGNMENT

- Assignment 4.1: Game Board Thumbnails (3–4) hours

2D Game Asset Pipeline Overview

We were introduced to the final project in Chapter 3, so now let's take a look at a high-level overview of a standard 2D game asset pipeline before we begin working on designing game-ready assets that will make up a personalized isometric game board. As mentioned previously, a game production, large or small, typically begins with a *game design document*, or *feature spec*, produced by the game design team, often with the input of the project management team. (*Note:* In later chapters, we will examine the specific roles of both 2D and 3D game development pipelines.) From there, the art team is tasked with visually translating this "wish list" into a visual target or concept. These initial stages of exploration are quick and loose, as the art team quickly generates several iterations of the asset(s) and also gathers reference materials (see Chapter 2) that will help to communicate a particular look or aesthetic. Next, after reviewing these early exploration images and appropriate references, a general direction will be approved by all major stakeholders (art director(s), producers, project managers, etc.), which then allows the artist(s) to move forward with completion of the art for the final in-game assets. While the 2D game pipeline can vary, assets are completed in either *bitmap* or *vector* format (see Chapter 2). Once art is complete, animation is

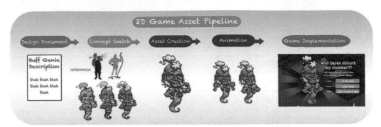

added if necessary. From this point, the completed art asset is handed off to a technical artist, whose job it will be to implement it into the game engine.

It's important to note that no two game pipelines are the same. They can vary not just from company to company but also from project to project. A smaller "start-up" game studio may ask an artist to wear multiple hats—for example, one day he or she may be generating concept art, and the next day he or she may be creating in-game vector art or animating with tools such as Adobe Animate. So, while it's important to be specialized to some extent as an artist, being familiar with the other aspects of game art creation such as a basic understanding of the game engine (Flash Player, Unity, etc.) that will be utilizing your assets and its various art creation/animation tools will make it easier for you as an artist to wear these multiple hats.

The Pitch

Now before we dive into the initial stages of asset creation, let's take a moment to examine what makes a strong pitch for any product. In all aspects of entertainment (including film, television, web, and gaming), there is an ever-growing need for creative content. As platforms and distribution channels evolve, your ability as a creator to produce this content (be it as an artist, writer, game designer, etc.) becomes incredibly valuable. However, as a creative person in the gaming industry, you will often be put in positions where you must pitch or "sell" your ideas and concepts to various "stakeholders" that, depending on your role within production, can run the gamut from immediate art director all the way up to the CEO of the company.

The ability to clearly convey your creative vision is vital as a visual designer, as the inability to do so can undermine even the most terrific of ideas or concepts. Prior to pitching any concept or idea, via a prepared presentation (PDF, PowerPoint, etc.) or an in-person pitch, there are a few things to keep in mind.

Know Your Audience

First, when pitching, ask yourself for whom is this product meant. Toddlers? Teenage boys? If it's the later, a simple fairy tale–esque story with a princess as the protagonist may not be the most appropriate. Ask yourself to whom you are pitching and what their market/audience is. For your own project, make sure to ask yourself, "Who is my audience?" Fellow students? Potential employers? Video game–loving friends? All of the above? A rough list of who you are targeting for your project will help establish a few broad parameters for your work. Mobile games producers in particular have begun to explore more focused demographic groups for their products. Previously the goal had been to target as broad an audience as possible (males and females from 7 to 70 years of age) with products in the "FarmVille/Candy Crush" mold, which are meant to be as simple to play and as colorful, appealing, and inoffensive as possible.

"FarmVille 2: Country Escape." (From Zynga, copyright 2009–2017. With permission.)

Recently, however, games focused on smaller targeted demographics have been shown to yield both higher retention and revenue. An example of a game for this more focused target demographic is Solstice Arena, which focuses on fighting mechanics and complex game controls.

"Solstice Arena." (From Zynga, copyright 2009–2017. With permission.)

Know Your Product

By approaching your creative endeavors as a "product," whether it's a simple spot illustration for a local newspaper or 3D feature animated film, you are immediately assigning value to it. Your work and ideas are intellectual properties that absolutely have value. In order to pitch them effectively, convincing yourself of this is the first step in also convincing a room of stakeholders of the value of your ideas. Know your product inside and out, everything from gameplay elements to visual targets to demographics. Where do you see your project fitting into the current market (be it games or film)? What are some similar properties? What are its competitors? How will you ensure you're bringing something unique to a specific genre or game type? If, for instance, you are doing a first-person shooter, in which the player has to fight his or her way through a zombie apocalypse, how have you differentiated it enough so that it is not just a knockoff of an existing property? These are all important questions that require you to first and foremost approach your work as that of a product.

Elevator Pitch

When pitching a game concept (or, for that matter, any entertainment industry project), it is crucial to have a simple written presentation, or elevator pitch, that sums up the project quickly and clearly. However, visuals are always more effective when it comes to grabbing your audience's attention. This is where your visual design skills become vital to any pitch—you need to create compelling imagery that immerses viewers in the world that your written documentation outlines. In pitches for new games, providing an "aspirational image" or "visual target" that represents what you hope to capture with the project is a must. (We'll also cover "aspirational images/visual targets" in later chapters, as they relate to marketing art). These images are meant to quickly sum up the bold beats of your project/product and should include everything mentioned previously.

Stakeholders (art directors, general managers, etc.) are busy folks and regularly listen to project pitches. Avoid falling into the trap of trying to explain every element of gameplay or the backstory of all your characters and their children. Try and limit a face-to-face pitch to between 5 and 15 minutes. Stick to the big picture; you should be able to describe the project convincingly in a sentence. Any great film or game can be summed up in one sentence, for example:

> *Star Wars*: A young farm boy joins the intergalactic rebellion against an evil empire armed with secret plans, quirky robots, and a mysterious connection to the Force.
>
> "Super Mario Bros.": A game in which the player(s) controls Mario and/or his faithful brother Luigi as he travels through the Mushroom Kingdom in order to rescue Princess Toadstool from the evil Count Koopula.

Attempt to boil your project down to similarly simple, straight-to-the-point descriptions, both in written and visual/aspirational forms. In the following, we have what became the visual target for "FarmVille 2" that was used to help sell stakeholders on the game pitch.

Note aspects of the image such as:

Tony Trujillo "FarmVille 2" Visual Target. (From Zynga, copyright 2009–2017. With permission.)

- A bright, saturated, yet natural color palette to indicate this is a grounded yet playful world

- Rounded and appealing shape design on everything from characters to animals to trees, evoking a friendly and inviting feel

- The presence of crops, tress, and animals to indicate a farming gameplay mechanic

- A "painterly" style of modeling for the various elements to suggest a 3D game development pipeline

In addition, when formulating a game pitch, it's often a good idea to include multiple style explorations within. Take note of how, in the explorations below, the styles represented:

- Are appropriate for the web/mobile game sector

- Evoke a different aesthetic/tone

- Allow the design to read across all variations

GRAPHIC   CEL-SHADED   PAINTERLY   RETRO/16-BIT

Hyoni Yim. (From Zynga, copyright 2009–2017. With permission.)

Initial Explorations: Thumbnails

Whether for the video game, TV/feature animation, or live-action entertainment industry *thumbnails* are often the first step toward zeroing in on a visual target, as they are meant to quickly communicate an idea by working initially at a small scale so as to eliminate detail and focus primarily on the "big picture" or "bold beat(s)" of a particular subject. Often this will include bypassing color and utilizing only a limited value scheme. Thumbnails for narrative mediums such as theatrical/TV animation are meant to quickly capture the mood of a piece, while also providing a variety of camera views, staging, and compositions that best communicate the information meant to be expressed in that particular "beat" or moment.

In the following, we have examples of traditional narrative thumbnails that were produced for television/film. Notice how the camera angles and compositions are varied while not overwhelming the sketch with unnecessary detail or color.

By comparison, with the thumbnail process as it applies to web and mobile games, and in this particular case your personalized "isometric game board," you'll be less concerned with camera

John Nevarez "Cinematic Thumbnails"

placement, as you will be working from a fixed isometric angle. We also already have some early asset concepts from the previous chapter's assignment that can be integrated into the thumbnails. Therefore, most of the artist's responsibilities will be establishing initial ideas for the game board background that will communicate setting/location, style, and aesthetic.

Ciaee Ching "Game Board Thumbnails"

The following thumbnail compositions have been completed with that fixed isometric angle and illustrate what is expected for this chapter's assignment, which will consist of six thumbnail designs focusing on the game board background of your personalized "isometric game board." The gameplay, or "live," area has been identified with a gridded box. This will represent where the individual assets such as characters, buildings, and props will reside (a process we began in the previous assignment). Everything beneath and outside of that will be considered your game board background.

Note how the artist has sacrificed refinement/details in favor of broad strokes that quickly communicate theme/design. As a result, the previous thumbnail's focus is on only that which is absolutely necessary in order to communicate the designs—*efficiency* and *clarity*. Color is not a priority at this stage and should not be addressed; however, a clear dominant light source, represented with a simple value scheme, is required because all of our game assets will eventually need to be executed with a consistent global light source to create a unified scene.

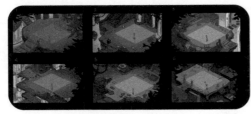

Florencia Kristiani "Game Board Thumbnails"

ASSIGNMENT 4.1   GAME BOARD THUMBNAILS (3–4) HOURS

Description

Using the initial exploration sketches, influence map, and reference library compiled in Chapter 3, begin thumbnails for your personalized "isometric game board" (six thumbnails total). Use your initial exploration sketches to populate the game grid area. The following images are representative of the minimum level of detail and finish recommended for game board thumbnail designs. One clear light source and a clear understanding of designing in an isometric environment are required. Look for variety of shape, design, and lighting between your six thumbnails.

Priorities:

- Limited detail

- Isometric perspective

- Clear global light source

- Communication of theme/setting

Alexandra DePasse "Game Board Thumbnails"

(*Continued*)

ASSIGNMENT 4.1 (CONTINUED)   GAME BOARD THUMBNAILS (3–4) HOURS

Game board Thumbnail Template

Media

There will be associated media.

Purpose

The purpose of this exercise is to complete a series of thumbnails that quickly establish the "big picture" of a personalized "isometric game board."

Materials

Traditional tools (pencils, pens, etc.)
   Adobe Photoshop

Conclusion

Upon completion of this chapter, you should have a high-level understanding of a 2D game pipeline, have examined what makes for an effective pitch, and be familiar with the initial game board thumbnail stage. Finally, you have also begun game board thumbnails for the personalized "isometric game board."

Quiz

4.1   Thumbnails are meant to focus on the "big picture" or "bold beat(s)" of a particular subject. T/F

4.2   All game development pipelines are the same. T/F

4.3   By approaching your creative endeavors as a "product," you immediately assign value to them. T/F

4.4   For any game pitch, providing an "aspirational image" is not necessary. T/F

Chapter 5

Visual Hierarchy

CHAPTER OBJECTIVES

In this chapter, we will define the concept of *visual hierarchy* and identify the various deliverables that will make up your final personalized isometric game board. We will also explore basic concepts relating to color theory in preparation for the development of your *color thumbnails.*

KEY LEARNING OUTCOMES

- Outline the deliverables for the personalized isometric game board.
- Define "visual hierarchy."
- Explore color as it relates to the creation of color thumbnails.

ASSIGNMENT

- Assignment 5.1: Game Board Color Thumbnails (3–4) hours

Final Project Deliverables, Part 1

Now that we've begun the initial stages of the final project—including establishment of the theme/aesthetic, reference gathering, and initial game board thumbnails—let's look a little closer at the specific deliverables and various asset types that will encompass the project outlined in the assignment section of each chapter throughout this book. The following image illustrates a rough overview of the various asset types that we will be designing and completing. It's important to note that these are all basic examples of assets/types and that specific categorization can vary from project to project in the web and mobile games industry. This list does, however, encompass assets/types that are common in many game development pipelines yet also leaves us plenty of room for customization for any theme or concept.

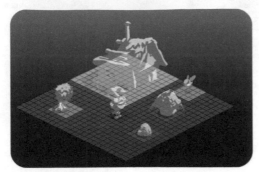

Game Board Asset Guide

Alexandra DePasse "Character Art"

Ciaee Ching "Big Buildable"

Previously, we have the basic template for the assets we'll be completing including:

- Characters (pink)

- Big buildable (green)

- Props (harvestable/destructible) (orange)

Characters: The personalized isometric game board will have two separate character assets, of which one will be your *avatar* (*player character*), which will be used to navigate the game board, and the second will be a *NPC* (*nonplayer character*), which can function as anything from a "helper" that assists the players progress to an adversary who impedes progress. We've already begun sketching out initial ideas for both of the characters (see the Chapter 2 assignment).

Big buildable: This asset will be the centerpiece of the game board and will function as a visual representation of a player's progress within the game. The big buildable will be required to have three states of progression and will be the largest individual asset on the game board. As noted previously, this asset's design is in no way limited to a building/structure. It can take shape as anything from an enchanted dragon to a postapocalyptic tank as long as it fits the specs provided, that is three progressive "states" and at least 8 × 8 (but not larger than 12 × 12) in tile size.

Project Deliverables, Part 2

Props: Our prop assets will be broken into two subcategories (*harvestables* and *destructibles*). In terms of size and appearance, these will be the same; however, the loose gameplay associated with each will differ slightly. Both, however, will require two "states" and will be no larger than 4 × 4 in tile size. *Harvestables*: These assets are meant to have a positive impact on the game board via providing elements useful to gameplay such as currency or energy. In the following example, we have a basic harvestable example in the form of a tree that produces fruit. Its two states are "bare" (state 1) and "mature" (state 2). This same functionality can be applied to anything from a treasure chest to an ani-mal/creature as long as it has two states that represent the bare/mature functionality and is no large than 4 × 4 in tile size. Typically, these assets can also be moved around the game board by the player for either decora-tive or efficiency purposes.

Harvestable

Destructibles: These assets are meant to impede a player's progression within the loose game design. An example is assets such as a boulder block-ing off a particular set of tiles, as this will require a player to smash or remove the boulder. In the following examples, a small tank and laser fence unit serve as the destructibles.

Juan Lopez "Destructible Art"

Background game board: We have also begun the initial stages of designing this back-drop that will establish the set-ting of our game board while also functioning as a fram-ing device for the individual assets described earlier (see Assignment 4.1). In traditional animation and live-action film, this would be similar to a lay-out or matte painting.

Ciaee Ching "Background Game Board"

Much of the rest of the content, tutorials, and assignments contained within this book will be structured around the design and completion of these assets, with two chapters dedicated to each: one for concept and one for completed asset.

Visual Hierarchy, Part 1

Next, we will be examining another important concept to keep in mind when approaching visual development for any type of imagery, whether for a video game, animation, or live-action film. We'll refer to this concept throughout this book—*visual hierarchy*. Establishing a visual hierarchy within an image, or in the case our game board, will be crucial in creating a well-organized and engaging composition for your viewers. While all video game screens are a collection of various art assets juxtaposed together, they are still meant to be engaged with visually as a singular image, no matter how many individual elements are present on screen at any given time. Therefore, the basic rules of visual design, such as clear *areas of interest*, still very much apply.

Eugene Delacroix "Liberty Leading the People." (Courtesy of Wikipedia, Liberty Leading the People, https://en.wikipedia.org/wiki/Liberty_Leading_the_People#/media/File:Eug%C3%A8ne_Delacroix_-_Le_28_Juillet._La_Libert%C3%A9_guidant_le_peuple.jpg, last modified on November 19, 2017.)

Let's first examine the following image, "Liberty Leading the People," by the artist Eugene Delacroix, and break down the visual hierarchy that has been established.

For this piece to work as well as it does requires a careful arrangement of elements by the artist, including value, composition, detail, and contrast. As you can see in the following, Delacroix has created a focal point by organizing his or her values and saturation levels in a way that the highest amount of contrast is on the figure holding the flag in the center of the composition (highlighted in pink).

Followed by the figure brandishing a pistol to the right of the focal point (highlighted in green) and finally working from the figures wounded in the foreground and up through the crowd to the left in the image (highlighted in orange).

Though you are working in an isometric perspective for your project's game board, these same concepts are required for any game screen. If overlooked, a game screen can become a jumbled experience that will not provide the viewer the proper visual breadcrumbs leading their eye clearly through an image.

Visual Hierarchy, Part 2

The following completed game board is an excellent example of strong visual hierarchy. In this example, the eye is immediately directed throughout the image in a way that both enhances and communicates the game's design and overall theme/aesthetic.

Ciaee Ching "Misty Village"

As we can see, by reserving the highest amount contrast of value and the highest level of saturation, the artist has directed the viewer's eye to the character avatar first (highlighted in pink).

The next asset we're led to, through the same control of contrast and saturation, is the large buildable asset (highlighted in green). As mentioned in this book's project guidelines, this asset is meant to act as a visual representation of the player's progress throughout the game, which is why it has the largest "footprint" on the game board. Next, we have the prop assets (destructables and harvestables) (highlighted in orange).

Note that for the game board background, the artist has considerably toned down both contrast and saturation (particularly around the edges of the image) in order to push the background back in the composition so as to adhere to the

concept of atmospheric perspective, which states as an object recedes further into space, contrast is lowered, temperatures are cooled, and saturation levels are reduced. As we can see, this is particularly effective in creating the illusion of depth in the image while also keeping the focus on the various game board assets.

Color Theory, Part 1

Color is a complex topic, and this book will not attempt to examine every aspect of the subject, as that is a book in and of itself. We will, however, provide a broad overview of color and examine how it can be properly utilized in casual web and mobile games.

Color is just one of several tools we will use to establish a strong visual hierarchy within a personalized isometric game board. Aspects of color—such as *hue, temperature,* and *saturation*—will be used to help direct a viewer's eye. Color on its own can be used to elicit emotional responses or imply a particular mood. Certain cool colors (blue, green, violet) can have a calming effect, while warm colors (red, orange, yellow) are active and can create a sense of excitement and warmth. These are very basic concepts that can be used to reinforce your project's concept/theme when applied to your game board.

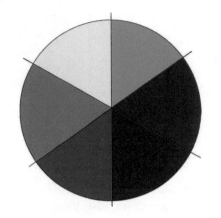

Following are a few important aspects of color:

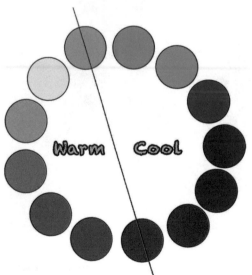

Hue is the property that allows a color to be identified as one of the twelve purest colors that make up the basic color wheel and include Primary (Red, Yellow, Blue), Secondary (Purple, Orange, Green), and Tertiary (red-orange, yellow-orange, yellow-green, blue-green, blue-violet, and red-violet).

Temperature (warm/cool): In the broadest sense, temperature is a method by which one can categorize different hues on a color wheel. Warm colors (red, yellow, orange) give a viewer the sense of energy or heat, while cool colors (blue, purple, green) give the viewer a sense of calm or stillness.

Temperature can describe the relationship between colors, but it can also describe the relationship of variations within a particular color; in the following two swatches, we see a cooler green and a green that appears warmer by comparison.

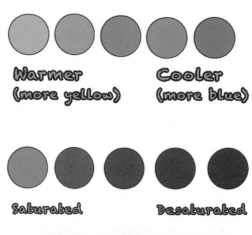

Saturation is often referred to as the intensity of a color, ranging from pure (100%) to gray (0%). A desaturated color is considered a dulled down take on a particular color.

Note: Value in particular will be a crucial element of our composition and needs to work in unison with our color palette. We will discuss in upcoming chapters how local value is impacted by lighting.

In the following image, note the use of saturation and temperature to guide the eye through the image. The highest amounts of both are reserved for the characters of the game—the lead character, Red, in particular, has the warmest temperature and the highest levels of saturation, instantly drawing your eye to him.

In the following isometric game board imagery, we see a similar controlled use of color where the player avatar character has both the highest amount of value contrast (flesh tone against his or her hair and suit) and saturation (which is fairly subtle, yet still present).

"Angry Birds." (From Rovio, copyright 2009–2017. With permission.)

"Adventureland." (From Zynga, copyright 2009–2017. With permission.)

"Dawn of Titans." (From Zynga, copyright 2009–2017. With permission.)

"Angry Birds." (From Rovio, copyright 2009–2017. With permission.)

Color Theory, Part 2

A specific color palette can also help to reinforce and communicate your theme's *tone*. For example, an action/fantasy game might utilize a desaturated palette with a low-key value scheme, communicating an aggressive/serious tone that reinforces the theme.

However, if the game's tone is meant to be upbeat and playful with broad appeal, then a saturated and bright, high-key palette would be fitting.

Color Thumbnails

For this chapter's assignment, you will be asked to select the two strongest initial game board thumbnails completed in Assignment 4.1. You will use these thumbnails to then complete two variations of color for each in preparation for completing the final background game board asset. Following are several examples. Notice that you will still be focusing on broad strokes and avoiding detail and refinement, as neither of which are a priority at this stage. Where shape and lighting were the goals in Assignment 4.1, color design will be the priority in this

Kim Truong "Color Thumbnails"

chapter. Keep it simple! Look to use basics of color we've covered in this chapter to help frame your individual assets. The goal is to capture the palette that will be most appropriate for the final game board. Experiment with several variations, as you never know when you will stumble upon a "happy accident" with your color choices. Keep in mind that you will be keying the rest of your assets off this background game board asset.

Chapter 6

Character Design, Part 1

> ## CHAPTER OBJECTIVES
>
> At this point in the project, we're going to set aside our background game board (don't worry, we'll come back to complete it in upcoming chapters) and move to the initial stages of designing the characters that will inhabit our project's world. As mentioned in the previous chapter, we will be completing two character assets: one player avatar and one NPC (nonplayable character). Character design—like several of the topics we've touched on thus far, including color theory and vector tools—is a dense subject that could take up an entire book of its own. Over the next several chapters, we'll look to boil it down to a handful of fundamentals that are crucial to consider when designing characters for any medium while at the same time identifying specific aspects of character design unique to the web and mobile game industry.
>
> ## KEY LEARNING OUTCOMES
>
> - Define the fundamentals of character design.
> - Identify how the fundamentals of character design relate to web/mobile games.
> - Begin the initial stages of vector character designs for your final project.
>
> ## ASSIGNMENT
>
> - Assignment 6.1: (2) Isometric Color Character Sketches (5–6) hours

Where to Begin

Before putting pencil to paper, we should start any character design by first asking our-selves a few quick questions:

- What is our character's role in the game? Is he or she the hero, villain, or helpful sidekick?

- What is our character's personality? Noble? Dysfunctional? Brutish?

- What aspects of the game design and/or storyline will impact the designing of our characters?

- Is our character male or female? Creature or humanoid?

- What colors identify the character? A friendly sidekick? A warmer palette might be appropriate. A villain? Perhaps consider a cooler desaturated palette.

- What's the character's body type—Thin, overweight, short, muscular?

After picturing the visuals of your character, it is also necessary to think about him or her in regard to the game production pipeline:

- Will this character be animated?

- Is it meant for a 2D or 3D production pipeline?

- If 2D, would vector construction be appropriate?

- What type of game engine will this character be presented in? An Adobe Flash–based engine? Unity?

These are all questions that will impact the how we approach and execute the design of any character. For example, if a character description begins with "a classic mad-scientist," portraying him as barrel-chested with handsome features (which is more in the traditional "hero" mold) wouldn't immediately come to mind.

Grant Alexander "Whack!" (BYXB)

There are no real "rules" with character design, outside of the fact that "Every element in a character design should be telling us something about them." Try to think of the loose parameters you (or your project's pipeline) lay out more as breadcrumbs that provide the viewer with a general sense of your overall design direction.

What Is Character Design?

So, what exactly is character design? Seems like a fairly simple question, right? Well, it is and it isn't. But, as mentioned earlier, there are several fundamental concepts that apply to all forms of character design, be it for a 3D animated feature, mobile video game, or professional sports mascot.

When breaking down any character design, we need to consider the following core aspects.

- Shape design

- Line quality

- Silhouette

- Volumetric versus Graphic

- Contrasting characters

- Color

Throughout the remainder of this chapter, we'll be exploring these concepts in detail.

Shape Design

The concept of shape language is one of the, if not *the*, most important aspects of character design, as our three basic   shapes (see the following) and the emotions they illicit are incredibly powerful when establishing the visual cues of your character's personality traits and role within a narrative.

Circles: Circles are typically used to convey *friendly, cute* characters. Circles have no acute edges, so they're ideal for capturing a soft, appealing personality such as the one exhibited by Reggie the Rat (see the following).

When establishing ages, the use of acute edges becomes important, as toddlers and young children typically are constructed using this concept, as they are friendly and appealing both physically (due to a layer of baby fat and lack of muscle definition) and emotionally (they have a positive, youthful outlook on life).

Squares: Squares communicate *stability* and *strength*. This shape is often used for the sturdy, heroic, and "heavy"-type characters (think club bouncer or trusty sidekick).

Triangles: The triangle is a very *active* shape, lending itself to more *sinister* or *suspicious* characters. Look to any classic animated film and you'll notice that the villains are comprised of primarily triangular shapes (eyes, noses, fingers, etc.)

Keep in mind that shapes are completely interchangeable and should be experimented with, as the combination of multiple shapes can convey complex and interesting personalities.

With the vampire-hunter character, we have a sturdy and powerful yet appealing combination of circles and squares that make up his or her build that are then accented by triangles throughout the costume (hat, coat, stakes, etc.), which in turn give the character an edgy/sinister quality.

Silhouette

A successful silhouette should provide a viewer with a solid amount of information about a particular character, as the silhouette will encompass a viewer's "first read." Take a look at the silhouette examples in the following. All read clear, creating a sense of personality and attitude through the poses, figure proportions, and shape design of each.

Graphic versus Volumetric

Another vital aspect of character design is the concept of "graphic versus volumetric." It's important to note that this is not an either/or decision. Think of it as more of a continuum with *graphic* at one end and *volumetric* at the other.

Within a graphic style, the designs are shape-driven. The designer is less concerned about indicating volume and form. As a result, the design tends to look "flatter."

Many current animated television shows (e.g., *Samurai Jack*) fall toward the "graphic" side of this continuum. These designs often utilize vector tools, which are then animated in programs such as Adobe Animate and Toon Boom while using "limited" animation techniques (which can be very cost effective from both a time and budget standpoint). The emphasis on shape and simplicity makes them ideal for the smaller scale (in contrast to the large-scale presentation of theatrical feature animation) at which they will be presented. For the same reasons, these types of designs can be incredibly effective on mobile and web gaming devices, which often utilize the same art and animation tools such as the aforementioned Adobe Animate and Toon Boom. And as we covered in Chapter 2, vector

GRAPHIC   *vs.*   **VOLUMETRIC**

(FLAT)   **(3D)**

art's typically smaller file sizes (compared to bitmap) make them even more optimal for many web and mobile game pipelines.

In contrast, when designing volumetrically, while the concept of shape design is still very important, there is added attention paid to establishing the illusion of depth and volume, such as with any traditional 2D or 3D animated feature film. These designs are often handed off to 3D modelers who bring them to life using programs such as Autodesk Maya, Max, or Z-brush (programs we will discuss further in upcoming chapters).

Contrasting Characters

When creating more than one character, keep in mind that they populate the same "world" and, as a result, should all share a similar visual style. A crucial step in ensuring that your characters play off each other well is to line them up next to one another. This gives you a great opportunity to compare and contrast everything from scale to line quality to color choices. Ideally, your characters will work to complement and contrast with one another. Consistency in style is a priority, but contrast (of shape, scale, etc.) is also important.

In the previous designs, note the contrast between the poses of the two characters—the character on the right is confidently leading with his or her chest, whereas the character on the left, in a much more relaxed pose, is leading with his (or her?) hips. Also note the added emphasis on triangles (angularity) of the character on the left (torn pant legs, shoulder spikes, etc.), the cooler color palette, and the obscured face. These details all make him or her appear more mysterious and slightly sinister when compared to the character on the right, who in turn appears more appealing and energetic due to the emphasis on rounder shapes (helmet, kneepads, etc.), chest out pose, and warmer/saturated color palette.

Using Color

Color should be used in the same way all the other elements of character design we've discussed are used—as a communicative device. All colors evoke specific emotions.

> *Red*: Passionate and sometimes dangerous. Also, due to its warm temperature, red will "come forward" more than any other color on the color wheel.

Blue: Generally cold and somewhat masculine. Blue is often associated with depth and stability.

Green: The color of nature. Green symbolizes growth, harmony, freshness, and fertility. Green has a strong emotional correspondence with safety.

These websites provide further details on the emotions specific colors evoke:

- http://www.incredibleart.org/lessons/middle/color2.htm

- http://www.color-wheel-pro.com/color-meaning.html

Ciaee Ching "Claus"

Putting the Concepts Together

The previously discussed fundamentals are all concepts that apply to any and all forms of character design. *How* they are applied can be project specific. Understanding and putting these concepts into effect will allow you to both lend credibility to and organize your designs in a way that makes clear to the viewer the "statement" you're attempting to make with your design.

Keep it simple ... but get as much information into the image as possible.

If we apply that same philosophy to the earlier character design, we can deduce that the character is:

- Friendly, based on his or her smile, circle-based shapes, and warmer color palette. He or she is also possibly a bit mischievous, with that accent of red from the bow tie.

- Smart and inquisitive, based on the large glasses and magnifying glass.

- Neat and organized, based on his or her well-maintained school uniform (royal blue) and the crisp, clean line quality that has been applied.

- Young, due to his or her proportions, large skull shape, and oversized bowtie and coat.

ASSIGNMENT 6.1   (2) ISOMETRIC COLOR CHARACTER SKETCHES (5–6) HOURS

Tools

Adobe Photoshop

Description

Complete color sketches for two characters in an isometric angle. You will need to design both your characters—one player avatar and one nonplayer character (sidekick, villain, etc.)—for your final project. You will be completing these with your vector tools in the next chapter, so it is important that you do all the "heavy lifting" in the bitmap sketch, including line work, color palette, and so on.

Florencia Kristiani "Color Character Concepts"

Florencia Kristiani "Color Character Concepts"

(*Continued*)

**ASSIGNMENT 6.1 (CONTINUED)   (2) ISOMETRIC COLOR
CHARACTER SKETCHES (5–6) HOURS**

You will need to complete sketches of four poses for each of your two characters:

1. Standard 3/4 "key" pose of both characters

2. "Front" idle in isometric
3. "Rear" idle in isometric
4. "Action" pose in isometric (look to show off each character's signature "move" or "power")

(*Continued*)

ASSIGNMENT 6.1 (CONTINUED)   (2) ISOMETRIC COLOR CHARACTER SKETCHES (5-6) HOURS

Purpose

Apply the fundamentals of character design to the concept sketch phase of the character assets for your personalized isometric game board.

Quiz

6.1 In basic character design, shapes are completely interchangeable and should be combined for more complex personalities. T/F

6.2 Red symbolizes growth, harmony, freshness, and fertility. T/F

6.3 Every element in a character design should be telling us something about that character. T/F

6.4 Circles are a very active shape, lending themselves to more sinister or suspicious characters. T/F

Chapter 7

Character Design, Part 2

CHAPTER OBJECTIVES

In Chapter 6, we were introduced to the fundamentals of character design, including *shape design*, *volumetric versus graphic*, and *contrasting characters*. In this chapter, we will further explore these fundamentals while also examining how they relate to web and mobile game development, including such topics as *line quality*, *leveraging stereotypes*, *model sheets*, and the translation of bitmap designs to *final vector game assets*.

KEY LEARNING OUTCOMES

- Continue to examine the fundamentals of character design.
- Leverage stereotypes within character design.
- Communicate a clear understanding of line quality.
- Explore the use of model sheets.
- Translate bitmap designs to final vector game assets.

EXERCISE/ASSIGNMENT

- Exercise 7.1: Character Model Sheets (1) hour
- Assignment 7.1: Final Vector Isometric Character Assets (5–6) hours

Angular (agressive)

Curve (smooth/appealing)

Curve/Angular

Rough

Line Quality

Line quality is another powerful communicative tool, as variation in line quality heightens descriptive potential while also adding to overall visual interest. Even when the subject or content of a drawing is not readily recognizable, line quality can imply texture, depth, movement, light, and so on. When the drawing is of a recognizable image, the types of lines you use can add to what you say about your subject matter by informing the overall mood for a viewer. Consider the types of marks (the line quality) in the images to the left.

Ask yourself, is the line quality used to describe your design smooth and friendly or rough and aggressive? Curved versus angular? Perhaps a combination of both? What's most appropriate based on the tone of the project and the target demographic?

The first image of the chicken (left) provides an example of the playful, family-friendly line quality that entertainment studios such as Disney often utilize, as it's marketable and appealing to all demographics.

Whereas in the second example, by applying a nervous/scratchy line quality to the same chicken design, we've adjusted the overall personality and attitude of the character. Compared to the playful, bouncy feeling of the first chicken, the second example comes off as asymmetrical and off—balance which are traits that often lend well to independent games and animation projects.

As far as the mobile games industry in general is concerned, there is a deliberate approach to create products that appeal to as wide an audience as possible and as result, the industry is primarily dominated by friendly, rounded shape- and line-based designs.

Stereotypes, Part 1

Stereotypes are typically a specific iconography (or caricature) that is recognizable to a general audience. A successful caricature exaggerates or distorts distinguishing features of a person or object to create an easily identifiable likeness, capturing its "essence" by boiling a design down to only the defining details. Common "character" examples include themes such as the outlaw cowboy, swashbuckling pirate, or film-noir femme fatale as these are instantly recognizable to an audience.

Let's think about what the key defining characteristics (icons/symbols) are that make a cowboy read visually as a "cowboy."

- Ten-gallon hat

- Western boots with spurs

- Chaps

- Six-shooter pistol

These are several visual cues that when used can immediately illicit the typical cowboy "feel" or personality in a character. Visualizing what specific collection of shapes make that silhouette unmistakably read as a particular stereotype is a helpful exercise when attempting to identify these cues.

Once you've established which iconography is at the root of a particular stereotype, you can apply such icons to any character for whose personality or role in a project they would be deemed appropriate.

Stereotypes, Part 2

The classic sea-faring pirate is another example of a well-known design icon (stereotype). There are endless variations of the "pirate"—just take a look at the complex cast of characters from some of the more recent high seas–themed Hollywood blockbusters—but let's ask ourselves what specifically is the iconography that ties them all together and makes us, the viewer, associate "pirate" with them?

Let's start with the silhouette:

Then focus in on a few particular elements:

- Triangular hat shape (think back to the feelings the triangle shape evokes)

- Curved blade swords (cutlass)

- Flintlock pistols

- Fold-over boots

- Diagonals, such as with the belts wrapping around the waist

- Peg leg

- Asymmetrical design

- Oversized ill-fitting clothing (gives them a very rugged, thrown together appearance)

- Loose items such as scarves and coat tails (look dramatic/cool when wind catches them)

Now the fun part when designing characters can be applying this established iconography to a design that falls outside of the typical fair such as with "Cecil the Cyborg" in the following, a bounty hunter from a far-flung steam punk future.

Remembering the fundamentals of character design that

we've been examining, we the viewer can ascertain quite a bit about this character's personality/attitude and his or her function in the story. We can surmise that this character is most likely nefarious in nature due to the pronounced triangle shapes throughout his design, cooler color palette, furrowed brow, and sharp angular weapons and features. Also, through the character's chest-out stance, we can surmise he's confident and most likely in a leadership position of some kind.

Stereotypes, Part 3

Keep in mind when tapping into established stereotypes that it's never enough to simply copy them. Use them as a foundation to then expand upon in order to create something unique. Oftentimes, it's more interesting to take accepted stereotypes and subvert them for dramatic/narrative effect. There are many successful examples of this in pop culture. Think of the classic "popular jock"—an antagonist that seems to occupy any story set in an educational environment from kindergarten to college. Let's examine our "Brock" character, who visually fits the classic hero mold (chiseled features, strong jaw, muscular build, etc.)

In the following image, however, we've subverted his design with a few subtle shifts such as the angularity and increased emphasis of the triangles in the eyes, chin, hair, and shirt collar. We've also desaturated his flesh tones and given his outfit a red/black costume color scheme of which we are hard-coded to recognize as meaning "danger" (black widows, poisonous snakes, etc.).

This subversion can be extremely effective when misleading an audience to a character's true intention. The trick, when subverting, is making sure to provide a visual breadcrumb trail for the viewers so that they don't feel cheated at the big reveal.

Paper to Pixel to Bitmap

Now that we have finalized our character designs in a rough bitmap form (see Assignment 6.1), we're now ready to move forward with our completed character assets. For this portion, we will be executing the final design utilizing the vector tools explored all the way back in Chapter 2. Advantages of completing our character assets with vector tools include:

- Vector art lends well to animation in most pipelines due to its lightweight nature.

- Their resolution independence means they can be displayed on multiple types of devices (computer monitor, tablet, mobile phone, etc.) without having to be reconstructed for each.

- The simple shape-driven aesthetic vectors provide reads well at a smaller scale presentation.

- As mentioned previously, the smooth, clean, simple nature of the tool lends well to the family-friendly, wide-audience appeal.

At this point in your character design stage, you should have the overall designs(s) locked down, including line work and color, so that you can move forward with the asset creation stage. Here you will utilize the tools and skills learned in previous chapters, utilizing the Photoshop vector tools to complete your final in-game character assets. The goal at this stage is to translate what should already be in bitmap form to a completed vector asset. If you've been thorough throughout the various steps of the design, such as color palette, lighting scheme, costume design, and shape design, this process should go relatively smoothly. If any of these elements are still to be addressed in your final vectors, you could be in for some frustration, as we've already found the tools themselves can be time consuming and do not lend well to quick iteration or to the "drawing/designing" stages.

Review the video media "Bitmap-Vector" for a more in-depth look at the tools we will be using to complete our final vector characters.

Character Model Sheets

Model sheets are incredibly important within any production environment, be it games or animation, and are the focus of our exercise for this chapter. Traditionally, they have been used by visual development artists to communicate the specifics of a character's design through refined line drawings, isolated expressions, character turns, color treatments, and whatever else might be necessary for the "downstream" disciplines, including animators, 3D modelers/animators, and so on, depending on the type of production (2D vs. 3D typically).

Kim Truong "Scarfari"

It's also important to note that a "character design" doesn't necessarily mean one drawing and can often consist of multiple drawings and paintings. Whatever is necessary to describe your design to your team, be it flash animator, 3D modeler, and so on, should be included.

For the purpose of this chapter's exercise, we will be looking to bring together your character design development work from previous chapters into one cohesive model sheet that will be an excellent addition to a portfolio. Following is an example of the layout you will be completing for each character.

EXERCISE 7.1   CHARACTER MODEL SHEETS (1) HOUR

Tools

Photoshop

Description

In this exercise, you will be arranging your development work, as shown in the following, in chronological order to emphasize the progression of your designs as you've completed them. When it comes to a visual development portfolio, it is important that you show your design process for your characters from initial sketch to completed asset.

Alexandra DePasse "Fox Frost"

Note: You will need to complete Exercise 7.1 prior to completing Assignment 7.1.

Purpose

Compile all design work for your characters into one portfolio-ready image.

ASSIGNMENT 7.1   FINAL VECTOR ISOMETRIC CHARACTER ASSETS (5–6) HOURS

Tools

Photoshop

Description

For this chapter's assignment, you will be translating bitmap color designs (completed in the previous chapter) to completed isometric vector game assets. You will be completing three states for each character, including *front idle, rear idle*, and *action* poses. You will be using the Photoshop vector tools explored in Chapter 2 to complete these assets.

Alexandra DePasse "Fox Frost"

Purpose

Apply the fundamentals of character design and a working knowledge of vector tools to your final project character assets.

Quiz

7.1   It's never a good idea to subvert a stereotype. T/F

7.2   Model sheets have traditionally been used by visual development artists to communicate the specifics of a character design. T/F

7.3   Stereotypes are typically a specific iconography (or caricature) that an audience associates with. T/F

7.4   Design questions should all be answered prior to the vector stage or our character asset creation. T/F

7.5   A good caricature captures the "essence" of a character. T/F

Chapter 8

Multistate Assets and Global Lighting

CHAPTER OBJECTIVES

Whereas in earlier previous chapters we've focused on the design and completion of our character assets, starting with this chapter, we will be switching gears and examining the design of our various "prop" assets, including our *big buildable*, *harvestable*, and *destructible* multistate assets. We will also discuss the importance of establishing a consistent *global light source* for the various elements within our isometric game board.

KEY LEARNING OUTCOMES

- Define the term "prop."
- Explore the concepts of consistency and variety.
- Identify the importance of a consistent global light source for a game board.
- Complete color concepts for prop assets.

ASSIGNMENT

- Assignment 8.1: Color Concepts for Props (3–4) hours

Multistate Assets

Over the next few chapters, we will be designing and completing final "in-game" art for several asset types that, for the purposes of this book, we will refer to as "multistate" assets. This simply means that while these are considered individual assets in the context of gameplay, the *in-game* visuals will consist of multiple versions or "states." Assets such as these are crucial for gameplay, as they work to drive engagement with players by representing such aspirational qualities as achievement, communicating information, and/or functioning as an appealing decorative element that adds visual interest to a game screen. For the purposes of the project, we'll tackle multistate "prop" assets of varying stages and sizes that will consist of three types:

- Big buildable

- Harvestable

- Destructible

What Exactly Is a "Prop"?

Before we begin the design stage of our various multistate prop assets, let's first look to define what exactly a "prop" is as it relates the games industry. In the broadest sense, a successful set of props provide the audience with key information about the world and its inhabits. This includes history, setting/location, and culture while at the same time reinforcing the overall design aesthetic (style) of a project.

Alexandra DePasse "Prop Designs"

In many cases, art pipelines consider any asset that is neither *character* nor *background* imagery (e.g., our background game board) to be a "prop." By definition, that can include everything from a bucket to a building (which means that our big buildable asset would technically be considered a prop as well).

Due to the varied size and complexity of props as well as the budget (time/money) required to complete them subcategorization is often necessary. These subcategories may include:

- *Small props*—Can include handheld weapons, tools, decorations, and so on

- *Complex props*—Those that require animation or are more complex in nature, including machinery with moving parts such as vehicles

- *Large props*—Can include buildings and large structures (e.g., big buildable)

Props: Harvestables/Destructibles

Harvestables

Harvestables fall into the "small props" sub-category, as they are both smaller in footprint (between 2 × 2 and 4 × 4) and made up of two states, which we'll refer to in generic terms as "bare" and "mature." In regard to the general game design of our project, this asset type will have a *positive* impact on gameplay, as it provides resources such as in-game currency and energy that players will use to progress throughout a game. The most common example of a harvestable is represented in the following with a simple plant/tree asset that bears fruit.

This basic functionality of "bare" and "mature" states can be applied to any number of concepts, from animals to enchanted wells, as long as the state fits the functionality of the asset type and is appropriate for your game theme/concept. In the following example, we have a message board with "bare" being empty of messages and "mature" represented by the posting of "clues," as the theme/concept involves detective work.

Ciaee Ching "Harvestable Art"

Destructibles

Destructibles are a prop asset similar to the previously discussed harvestables in both "footprint" size and number of states (between 2 × 2 and 4 × 4 footprint and two states). What differentiates the destructibles and harvestables is purely the context of the rough game design. Whereas harvestables are meant to have a positive impact on the

game board, destructibles will in turn have a negative impact, which can be represented as an obstacle that impedes movement of the player's avatar or progression such as a large boulder that must be broken down in order to pass through a particular area on the game board.

Note: Variations of the earlier multistate assets populate most game development pipelines and can be referred to by differing terminology depending on the company/project.

Alexandra DePasse "Fox Frost"

Consistency

As we begin designing our props, maintaining consistency between our various asset types (props, characters, and background game board) is of utmost importance. This can be achieved a number of ways, including:

- Color palette

- Consistent line quality

- Global lighting

- Style treatment (see Chapter 10)

- Materials (wood, precious metals, etc.) (see Chapter 10)

Note: As you can see in several of the examples, for the sake of variety in the final game board, props can include creatures/animals. Normally, these would be given their own category within a pipeline; however, for the purposes of simplification and variety of assets, we'll group them with the general "props" within our game boards.

Color Palette

When approaching the overall color palette for props, we can use the other completed (characters) and in-progress (background game board color concept) assets as a jumping off point. Ideally we are selecting colors that support our theme's mood, subtly communicate the functionality of the prop (harvestable or destructible), and complement the background game board asset.

The arrangement of hue/temperature is an effective strategy when organizing color choices. For example, reserving warmer colors (and a more rounded shape design) for the harvestables clearly communicates the *positive* nature of the asset on the gameplay progression.

On the other hand, reserving acute angles and a palette weighted toward the cooler end of the spectrum can be effective in communicating the destructible's *negative* impact on gameplay.

Variety

While we've stressed the importance of *consistency* with our assets, another concept that is crucial is the idea of creating *variety* amongst our assets in order to avoid repetition.

Consistency creates unity; variety creates interest in an image.

With your props, due to collision limitations (4 × 4), the easiest way to ensure a sense of variety is with the silhouette shape of your assets. As you can see in the following, even though the assets will be relatively close in size (footprint), there are a wide variety of shapes that can be used to create variety and communicate that simple functionality (havestable/destructible).

Note: In addition, as it can assist in providing variety for the game board, we will discuss the differing of "finish" style for our assets in Chapter 11.

Progress Question

You should maintain consistency in your _____ , as well as in your theme/concept.

    a.   color palette
    b.   line quality
    c.   style treatment
    d.   all of the above

Florencia Kristiani "Prop Designs"

Visual Cue

As was mentioned early in this chapter, props should also function as a visual cue and tell viewers as much as possible about the world/narrative/inhabitants you're creating for your characters and other assets. Your props, and really any asset on your game board, should be designed to use materials, technology, and culture to provide a player with information about and insight into the world being brought to life.

If, for instance, your game board setting is the often-used design trope "fantasy," using materials and technology from an old-world aesthetic would be appropriate for your props, as this theme tends to utilize design language from the past. Commonly sourced periods for elements such as fashion, architecture, tools, and weapons include classic antiquity, medieval, and Victorian. This recognizable and functional approach helps to ground the outlandish "magical/fantastical" aspects of the theme (inorganic colors, objects defying gravity, etc.) and render them relatable and recognizable.

Global Light Source

As we begin the design stage of our props, establishing a clear global light source within the game board is a vital step in ensuring all the various game board assets composite as a unified scene, while also reinforcing the illusion of dimension and depth in your environment.

So, how do we establish that global light source? The trick is in a consistent approach to the cast and form shadows of all the various elements. As the following guide illustrates, the shadows of all our various assets should be lit by the same directional light source. As a result, the form and cast shadows should all be consistent with that directional light source. In the following guide, notice how the light source is roughly at the 1 p.m. position, resulting in the arrangement of all the shadows (including form and cast shadows) that is slightly more toward the left-hand side of the asset.

For the sake of this example, notice that all cast shadows are a solid black set to 35% transparency. The transparency ensures that the value mixes with the underlying game board colors to further sell the sense of illusion of depth and the "grounding" of assets.

For your own isometric game board, your primary light source (sun, moon, enchanted gem, etc.) should be arranged between 10 a.m. and 2 p.m. on the clock face.

However, exceptions to the universal cast shadow values (in this case, black at 35% opacity) can be made. One example where an exception could be made would be with assets that do not touch the ground, or hover, such as in the following example. In this asset's case, the transparency of the black cast shadow has been adjusted from 35% to 15% to sell the idea that the asset is hovering off the ground plane. As in nature, a cast shadow will lighten the further away from an object it is and works as a subtle reinforcement of that illusion of depth.

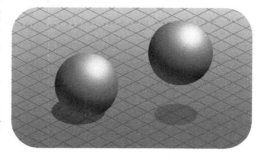

ASSIGNMENT 8.1   COLOR CONCEPTS FOR PROPS (3–4) HOURS

Tools

Adobe Photoshop

Description

In this assignment, you'll be completing the color concepts for all four of your prop assets (harvestables/destructibles). You will need to design both your harvestables (positive impact) and destructibles (negative impact) for your final project. You will be completing the final game-ready assets in Chapter 10, so it's important to do all the "heavy lifting" in the bitmap sketch, including line work and color palette.

Florencia Kristiani "Prop Color Concepts"

Alexandra DePasse "Prop Color Concepts"

Purpose

To utilize the concepts of design to create a variety of prop assets that are both interesting and consistent in their design aesthetic while also providing visual cues to the history, culture, and technology of the game's world.

Quiz

8.1   Shadows on various assets should never be lit by the same light source. T/F

8.2   The basic functionality of bare and mature states can be applied to any number of concepts. T/F

8.3   Destructibles have a negative impact on the game board. T/F

8.4   For the purposes of this course, props encompass harvestables, destructibles, and the big buildable assets. T/F

8.5   Props should never function as visual cues to inform the world/narrative. T/F

Chapter 9

The Big Buildable

CHAPTER OBJECTIVES

In this chapter, we'll be completing the color concept stage of our large multistate prop asset in the form of the *big buildable*. We'll also explore the basic fundamentals of lighting such as intensity, hard versus soft, and dynamic. Finally, we'll complete a game board "gut check" image consisting of all of our current in-progress assets.

KEY LEARNING OUTCOMES

- Understand the various qualities of light as they relate to the isometric game board and the gaming industry in general.
- Express a basic understanding of dynamic lighting and how it affects the art asset creation process.
- Complete color concepts for the big buildable asset.

EXERCISE/ASSIGNMENT

- Exercise 9.1: Game Board "Gut check" (1) hour
- Assignment 9.1: (1) Big-Buildable Color Concept (5–6) hours

Intensity

Continuing the discussion begun in the previous chapter regarding global lighting, when the subject of a light source's *intensity* is discussed, it is in reference to the brightness and measured rate at which light falls upon an object from any given source. The intensity of

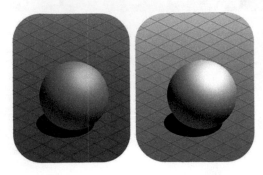

your light source will play a valuable role in determining specific aspects of your scene/game board such as time of day, location, and overall mood and tone.

Consider the following variation of intensity between sunlight (right) and moonlight (left) as it applies to global lighting. While moonlight is cooler in color temperature, the overall value contrast is much lower than the light emitted from the sun.

Light Quality

Equally important is the overall *quality* of your light. To simplify things, we will divide this aspect into two categories—*hard light* and *soft light*.

Hard Light

Hard lighting is characterized by a strong, bright, directional light. An object lit by a hard light source (such as a spotlight) casts sharp, crisp shadows (both form and cast) that correspond with the directional light source. Hard lighting is typically a very dramatic lighting scheme that can create a chiaroscuro effect (strong/dramatic tonal contrast of lights and darks). Contrast, as you recall, is one of our most effective tools when organizing our isometric game board's visual hierarchy. This light quality will be ideal for various individual assets, as it prioritizes contrast and reinforces the global lighting via form and cast shadows.

Soft Light

Soft lighting tends to be of a more diffused quality and falls on the subject from multiple directions in a more *sculptural* manner. The directional light of an object is not always as clear as "hard" light, thus giving the cast shadows softer edges.

This *sculptural* lighting can be particularly effective for secondary or "static" assets such as marketing imagery (which will be covered in detail in Chapter 12) for reasons including the lack of distinct directional lighting provides the ability to composite, rearrange, and reuse multiple assets (characters, props, etc.) within a scene (see the image to the left).

Soft lighting, with its low contrast and uniform directional light, allows for these assets to be moved freely within this composition (as well as others) without the artists having to adjust the shadows and lighting. This lighting is also ideal for concept art to be used for the informing of 3D models, as it prioritizes form and local colors (see Chapter 12).

Tony Trujillo "FarmVille 2." (From Zynga, copyright 2009–2017. With permission.)

Combining Light Qualities

With the previous in mind, we should look to take advantage of the concept of hard light versus soft light when reinforcing the visual hierarchy within a game board.

In the following example, take note of how the artist has utilized a soft lighting approach (in relation to the rest of the game board assets) for the background game board asset (which we're still in the stages of completing for our own game board). This is a conscious choice on the designer's part in an attempt to push the background back while also emphasizing the mysterious

Ciaee Ching "Background Game Board"

and "misty" atmosphere that his or her game theme/concept indicates in the name, "The Riddle of Misty Village."

Progress Question

With soft lighting, light can fall on an object from multiple directions.
    True/False

Ciaee Ching "Completed Game Board"

Dynamic Lighting

Dynamic lighting is a technique that simulates realistic or "active" lighting within a game scene in real time, as opposed to a game artist including the lighting effects directly into the various assets (as we've been doing up to this point). This allows for the lighting of the game world to respond to realistic envi-

"Dawn of Titans." (From Zynga, copyright 2009–2017. With permission.)

ronment changes such as location, time of day, and weather conditions without having to create additional art assets for each (which when multiplied across a large number of assets begins to be inefficient from a production standpoint). The drawback, however, is that *dynamic lightning* is computationally expensive, and many such games require a powerful computer in order to take advantage of its benefits.

As a result, dynamic lighting has primarily, until very recently, been reserved for console games, whereas PC/mobile games "bake" or include shadows (form and cast) within the art assets to save processing power. For the purposes of our game board, as it is a 2D art pipeline that we've been designing for, shadows and lighting have

"Empires and Allies." (From Zynga, copyright 2009–2017. With permission.)

been included in the asset art. It is important to note, however, that industry trends are changing due to technological advancements. Dynamic lighting is becoming increasingly common for PC and mobile game pipelines. Games such as Empires and Allies utilize 3D models in their game development pipelines that allow for dynamic lighting when it is cost effective.

After having completed the color concepts for our small prop assets (harvestable/destructible) in the previous chapter, we'll now turn our attention to the color concepts for our large *prop big buildable* asset (Assignment 9.1). Once completed, we'll then assemble our game board "gut check" (Exercise 9.1), which will consist of all our various assets composited together for review purposes.

"FarmVille - Haunted Hallow." (From Zynga, copyright 2009–2017. With permission.)

Anna Parmentier "FarmVille 2." (From Zynga, copyright 2009–2017. With permission.)

The Big Buildable

We mentioned previously (see Chapter 5) that the big buildable's function is that of the "centerpiece" of the isometric game board (as shown in the following image), as it serves as a visual representation of a player's progression within the game.

As it is your centerpiece, the big buildable will have both the largest footprint on the game board (a maximum of 12 × 12), while also containing highest total number of states—three. This means that you will need three separate pieces of art that emphasize clear *progression* and *upgradability* from state to state for this one asset. Balance among your asset's state progression is crucial because you want to clearly show the aspirational quality of progressions, which will in turn encourage players' continued engagement with the game feature that the big buildable asset is assigned to.

The images to the left and below are examples of the big buildable asset type. All three examples include three states of progression, a consistent footprint, and an increase in height and complexity between stages, all of which communicate the sense of player progress/achievement.

Take particular note of how, despite the variation of silhouette and scale of the states (particularly between the first and second stages in the following), the artist has visually tied them together with the use of similar materials, color palette, and props across all three states of the buildable.

Keep in mind that as it relates to the assignment outlined in this chapter, you are by no means required to design a "building" for the big buildable asset. In place of this asset, an artist could design anything from a child's clubhouse.

To a treasure hoarding dragon.

As long as it meets the basic require-

Sarah Ortiz "Big Buildable"

ments of the asset type—it must be the largest individual asset on the game board (no bigger than a 12 × 12 footprint) with a three-stage progression.

Gut Check

To recap, at this point in your project you should have all of the following assets either completed or in progress:

- One Background game board—in progress color rough

- Two characters (avatar/NPC)—completed

- One 3-stage big buildable—in progress color rough

- Four small props (harvestable/destructible)—in progress color rough

In an effort to ensure consistency of style (color palette, line quality, shape design, etc.) within our game board, we'll assemble our various in-progress assets onto one "gut check" image at the conclusion of this chapter. This will give you an opportunity to spot any inconsistencies and make any necessary adjustments prior to the completion of the various in-progress assets that make up your personalized isometric game board.

Alexandra DePasse "Gut Check"

EXERCISE 9.1   GAME BOARD "GUT CHECK" (1) HOUR

Tools

Adobe Photoshop

Description

For this exercise, you will compile all of your assets, in their various states of completion, together on your work-in-progress (WIP) game board. This will provide an opportunity to check for issues regarding the consistency/unity of various elements of your overall game board, including:

- Color palette
- Line quality
- Shape design

Use the template provided to compile assets and present your WIP game board for feedback.

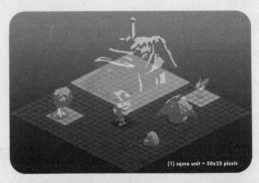

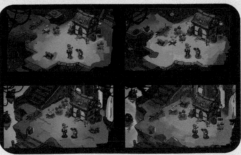

Florencia Kristiani "Gut Check"

(*Continued*)

EXERCISE 9.1 (CONTINUED)   GAME BOARD "GUT CHECK" (1) HOUR

Media

Download: **asset_scale_guide.psd**.

ASSIGNMENT 9.1   (1) BIG-BUILDABLE COLOR CONCEPT (5–6) HOURS

Tools

Adobe Photoshop

Description

For this assignment, you will be completing color roughs of all three stages of your big buildable. Keep in mind that these are "roughs," so smaller details and polished rendering are not the priority. It's important at this stage to not overcommit to the earlier in case adjustments or further concepts are necessary based on feedback from an art director. A simple clear line drawing, local color, and a simple directional light source is all that will be necessary at this stage.

Examples

Alexandra DePasse "Big Buildable Color Concept"

(Continued)

ASSIGNMENT 9.1 (CONTINUED) (1) BIG-BUILDABLE COLOR CONCEPT (5–6) HOURS

Kim Truong "Big Buildable Color Concept"

Purpose

Design color roughs of a cohesive/progressive three-stage asset that can be used to complete the final big buildable game asset.

Media

View video media "Big Buildable."

Quiz

9.1 Soft lighting is a technique that simulates realistic real-time lighting. T/F

9.2 Intensity is the amount of light that falls upon an object from a light source. T/F

9.3 Hard lighting tends to be of a more diffused quality than soft lighting. T/F

9.4 The big buildable will act as the "centerpiece" of the game board. T/F

Chapter 10

Prop Design (Continued)

CHAPTER OBJECTIVES

In this chapter, we'll continue to develop our various "prop" assets (which include both *harvestables* and *destructibles*) by expanding on the concepts introduced in Chapter 9 such as hard versus soft lighting and how they impact our completed assets. We'll also explore a few basic approaches to rendering our props. Finally, we'll explore working with graphics and the proper scaling of our completed assets.

KEY LEARNING OUTCOMES

- Understand basic rendering techniques in Adobe Photoshop.
- Understand proper final assets scaling.
- Complete prop assets.

ASSIGNMENT

- Assignment 10.1: Completed Prop Assets (5–6) hours

Asset Cohesiveness

As we work to complete our various *prop* assets, keep in mind that with your approach to rendering (whether a more "painterly" or "graphic" finish), details such as material

Brandon Pike "Loading Dock Concept." (From Zynga, copyright 2009–2017. With permission.)

Florencia Kristiani "Completed Harvestable Prop"

and texture will need to match the overall level of stylization of the design from a shape/form standpoint. For example, if the reference for a wood texture contains detail such as notches or grain, then those will need to be simplified to fit the same level of stylization as the rest of the design.

With complex or repetitive details such as the earlier wood planks that make up a flooring, make sure to ask yourself whether three shingles would be more readable at our smaller game scale than the five shingles in the reference image. And if there is important texture information that needs to be applied, could you enlarge/simplify (or even eliminate) that texture to emphasize readability and simplicity?

It's these smaller decisions that will ensure a consistent look/style to your designs no matter the "finish."

Keep in mind as you move to complete your various assets that the only asset type vector tools have been utilized for thus far in your project are the "character" assets (player avatar/NPC). Experimenting with a variety of finishes for the remainder of the assets is absolutely encouraged, and as stated in the previous chapter:

Consistency creates unity; variety creates interest in an image.

This variety can take the form of the aforementioned "finish" applied to your various assets. In the following example, examine the varying "finishes" applied to the individual props.

Whereas a "painterly finish" can utilize a more *soft lighting* approach with its subtler rendering (left), a "flat-color/vector finish" (right) can resemble a *hard lighting* approach with its sharp, shape-driven rendering (see Chapter 9).

Basic Rendering

As we move into the completing of our various *prop* assets it would be a good time to explore a few of the tools available to us in Adobe Photoshop and a basic approach to rendering.

Quick Tips

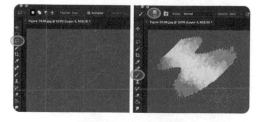

- *Lasso tool*—The best painting tool in Adobe Photoshop is actually not a brush but in fact the lasso selection tool, as it (similar to the vector tools we've previously discussed) requires a shape-driven approach to design. By "lassoing" shapes and then using your various brushes to fill, you're able to paint graphically.

- *Brushes*—Try and limit yourself to only a few rendering brushes (one or two are more than enough). The following "evil pumpkin" example was completed using one brush for everything, from the line drawing to the rendering.

- *Layer blend modes*—Utilize layer blend modes and image adjustment tools for contrast and value arrangements.

Line and Local Color

Starting off with a loose, but clear, line drawing combined with local color (make sure that your local or "base" color isn't too bright initially in order to allow for mid-tone/highlight application). We effectively completed this step in Assignment 8.1. *Important: Make sure you're using separate layers for each step described and that your line work is placed on the top layer in the layers palette.*

Shadow Shape

Design a shadow shape with the lasso selection tool based on the direction of the global light source. For this particular stage, an approach that can be particularly effective is leveraging *layer blend modes* native to Adobe Photoshop such as "*multiply*." This setting both *darkens* and *mixes* the underlying color consistently across multiple materials (pumpkin skin, leaves, etc.) by using one "shadow color"—in this case, muted purple.

We must also make sure to clearly define *cast* (hard edge circled in green) versus *form* (soft edge circled in red) *shadow edge quality*. This stage is important, as it gives the asset a "painterly" appearance. When you want to depict form shadows, a texture brush of your choice may come in handy.

Mid-Tones

Apply mid-tones to the "light" areas based on directional light. Look to use a warm/cool relationship of color, as for this particular asset we're using a basic warm light (sunlight), which is represented by the yellow/orange swatch. Again, *layer blend modes* will come in handy when blending your lighting across multiple materials; in the case, we'll use "*overlay*," which will *mix* and *brighten* the underlying color.

Highlights

Work within mid-tones to push brighter values as on the object depending on the level of specularity (shininess). In this case, the surface of the pumpkin is "shinier" than the leaves. As a result, an additional layer of highlights (*layer blend mode—overlay*) will help communicate this and create specular variety.

Polish/Refinement

At this stage, our focus is on adjustments to aspects such as color and contrast using the *color balance* (*image—adjustments—color balance*) and *levels* (*image—adjustments—levels*) options while also adding additional details such as a cast shadow on the ground plane, bounce light on stalk, and secondary glow effects.

The amount of details added are up to the individual artist; however, keep in mind that the subtler these additions are, the less likely they will be seen and appreciated at the web/mobile game scale.

This basic approach can be used for any type of asset, including the smaller props we'll be completing in this chapter and complex assets such as the *big build-able* (which we'll be completing in the next chapter).

Visual Hierarchy and Cast Shadows

If we were to stack rank assets in terms of their importance to the game board's visual hierarchy, we would have:

- Character avatar/NPC

- Big buildable

- Harvestable/destructible

- Background game board art

One simple method of reinforcing the visual hierarchy listed earlier is to adjust the cast and form shadows of your various assets so that they slightly differ in value contrast. This manipulation of contrast subtly emphasizes the importance of your characters and big buildable assets over your destructibles/harvestables. Adjusting the cast shadow is fairly easy, as we're using simple solid black shapes to represent them; however, adjusting contrast for form shadows can be a bit more time consuming. One recommendation is that within your working source file, you can clearly separate your shadow layer (as we've done based on the previous rendering workflow) from the rest of the art, as this will allow for easier adjustment of shadow intensity. When handled properly, this can be very effective in reinforcing that well-organized visual hierarchy.

In the image to the left, take note of the subtle adjustment of contrast in the form and cast shadows of each asset type: character (left), big buildable (center), and harvestable/destructible (right).

Working with Graphics

As up to this point we've been producing our assets with the idea that they will inhabit a typical 2D game engine, there are several aspects of the preparation of your art we need to address. First, it's important to have an understanding of the requirements for your game's particular pipeline in order to have your art in the best shape possible for easy implementation by a developer or for animation by an animator.

As artists, it's easy to approach our work with the attitude that once we've finished the art on an asset, that work is then done. *Nothing could be further from the truth.*

In any game pipeline, as an artist, you will be tasked with handling varying amounts of technical art duties, depending on several factors, including your game's platform (mobile, PC, console), engine (Unity, Unreal, HTML5, etc.), and the size of your team. Whether it's something as simple as exporting transparent PNG's from your PSD source files—to the proper naming conventions of your files—to migrating your work to a version control software (such as Perforce or SVN), exposing yourself as an artist to the various disciplines within a game development pipeline is crucial and immediately makes you that much more vital to

a development team (we'll be exploring these other disciplines over the next few chapters). An important thing to remember is that any organization is better than none, and the complexity of a project often dictate the best structures to use.

Typically for a non-animated asset or "static" asset, such as your props, you will submit your game art in a bitmap format, which more often than not is a transparent PNG. Depending on the engine your game utilizes, a developer or technical artist (a sort of hybrid developer/artist that works as a conduit for the two disciplines) will input a set of values for that particular asset in order to communicate that asset's render size in the game. As we've already discussed, bitmap formats do not scale well without a degradation of quality. Consequently, exporting your final PNG file at the correct "in-game" size is crucial to ensure that your final assets are presented in the best possible quality. For example, if your prop asset is meant to be a 3 × 3 collision on the game grid, the width of the asset would be 150 pixels across. We get this pixel count by adding the x and y values of the footprint (3 × 3 is 3 + 3 = 6). We then multiply that by 25 pixels (6 × 25 px = 150 px). So in effect, your prop should be 150 pixels across when submitted as a final asset.

What about a 4 × 4 footprint? 4 + 4 = 8.

8 × 25 px = 200 pixels across. Simple, right?

As all game development pipelines differ, keep in mind that identifying and navigating these nuances within the pipeline are crucial to your success as a game artist. Nothing will frustrate your coworkers more than indifference as to how your work fits into the overall game.

For the purpose of this project, you will create transparent PNGs for all your asset states at their appropriate pixel dimensions. You will then replace your "color concepts" with your final rendered assets in assetscaleguide.psd we set up in Exercise 9.1: Game Board "Gut check" (1) hour.

ASSIGNMENT 10.1   COMPLETED PROP ASSETS (5–6) HOURS

Tools

Adobe Photoshop

Description

Complete final art for all four of your multistate prop assets (harvestables/destructibles) using either the vector tools covered in Chapter 2 or the bitmap rendering techniques covered in this chapter. Make sure to keep both the consistency of your game board's art style and visual hierarchy in mind. Once completed, export individual assets as the properly sized PNGs (which was covered in this chapter's "Working with Graphics" section) and replace your "color concepts" within your "Gut Check" PSD file (which was assembled in Exercise 9.1 "Game Board Gut Check (1) Hour").

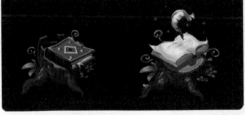

Conclusion

In this chapter, we continued to develop our prop assets (which include both *harvestables* and *destructibles*) by exploring rendering techniques and expanding on the concepts introduced in Chapter 9 such as *hard versus soft lighting* and how these aspects impact our completed assets. Finally, we examined working with graphics and the importance of proper scaling for our final assets.

Quiz

10.1   Final assets must all be completed with the vector tool. T/F

10.2   The lasso selection tool must never be used for painting in Adobe Photoshop. T/F

10.3   The layer blend mode "Multiply" darkens and mixes the underlying color. T/F

10.4   Adjusting the cast and form value contrast can subtly reinforce your game board's visual hierarchy. T/F

Chapter 11

Art Team Roles and Collaboration

CHAPTER OBJECTIVES

In this chapter, we'll take a closer look at the various art roles within a 2D game art team and the disciplines with which the art team collaborates in a game development pipeline. In addition, we'll complete our large prop asset, "the big buildable," using the basic rendering concepts introduced in Chapter 10.

KEY LEARNING OUTCOMES

- Further define the various roles within a 2D game pipeline art team.
- Define other disciplines with which the art team collaborates.
- Complete final art for the "big buildable" prop asset.

ASSIGNMENT

- Assignment 11.1: Completed Big-Buildable Prop Asset (5–6) hours

Production Overview

Where in Chapter 4, we took a high-level look at an art asset production pipeline, in this chapter, we will be taking a step back from the specifics of visual design (character design, global lighting, etc.) in order to examine the various positions within a typical art team and the disciplines they interact with on a day-to-day basis within a game development environment.

Art, much like technology, is evolving at a lightning-fast pace (which is why in Chapter 10, we emphasized the need to be nimble/versatile as a game artist). As projects scale in size and complexity (such as with the introduction of 3D graphics), the types of roles for artists evolve/scale with them. Job titles will be added and fragmented into multiple roles that can be specialized in nature and until recently, it was not uncommon for a "game artist" to be responsible for the *concept, production, animation,* and *implementation* of a particular asset. Again, depending on the size and budget of a project (and whether it's a 2D or

3D art pipeline), this can still be the case. Keeping in mind that our current project is being built around a traditional 2D production pipeline, let's look a little closer at some of the various job titles within an art team.

Associate/Junior/Intern Artist

For those in an entry-level position and new to the games industry (such as recent higher education graduates), some variation of the above section name will be their title. These artists generally handle simpler tasks such as reference gathering for the team, bug fixing (addressing issues with individual assets), limited asset design (small props being an obvious choice)—and are generally looking to gain valuable experience while proving their reliability to the production team.

Concept Artist

A concept artist's job is that of being the first artist to execute designs for characters, creatures, environments, and objects for the world the game design team has mapped out in the initial game design document. The entire look of the game is typically keyed off of the initial concepts (rough paintings, drawings, etc.) that a concept artist produces, upon approval of all major stakeholders (art director, lead game designer, etc.). As mobile/web games are "live" games (i.e., they are ongoing once launched), a concept artist continues to visually flesh out new features and assets that will be introduced within the game, after which the production artists will complete the final assets, whether they be 2D bitmap/ vector assets or 3D models.

Grant Alexander "Whack! Background Concept" (BYXB)

"Kicker Character Concepts"

Production Artist

The role of production artist can encompass a large variety of art skills and digital tools, including 2D (Photoshop, Illustrator, Adobe Animate) and 3D (Maya, 3D Studio Max, ZBrush). But generally, a production artist uses the work established by the concept artists as blueprints/inspiration to bring to life the final in-game assets. For instance, a concept artist might put together an image encompassing a scene/game board. The various production artists would be tasked by the art director or lead artist with the execution of individual final game assets (props, characters, etc.) based upon that concept art.

Final 2D Game Assets

Grant Alexander "Completed Whack! Items" (BYXB)

Grant Alexander "Completed Whack! Background" (BYXB)

Art Lead (Senior Artist)

An art lead's role can vary; however, in essence, he or she is meant to be an extension of the art director. An art lead is responsible for maintaining consistency in both the *style* and *quality* of art all while maintaining a role in the production of assets. Limited personnel management may be required in some cases (such as managing junior members of the art team). As a production scales in size, art leads become increasingly important to have in place, as in some cases there can be upward of hundreds of assets in production at any given time. This volume of assets would be overwhelming for a single art director; he or she would not be able to take the appropriate time to scrutinize and guide them from concept to final asset.

Lead structure can be assigned by specific art *discipline* or *asset type* at different times to oversee production.

Leads by Discipline:

- Animation lead

- Marketing art lead (promotional art, ads, etc.)

- Concept art lead

- Outsource lead (coordinate with offsite vendors)

Leads by Asset Type:

- Decorations/props lead

- Buildings lead

- Animals lead

- Avatar/NPC lead (all humanoid characters)

Art Director

The art director is ultimately responsible for all the aspects of an art team, including maintaining a consistent style and managing personnel such as the associate, concept, and production artists. An art director must have a solid grasp on all aspects of the creation of the art (concept, production, animation, etc.), must have strong communication skills, and must understand the project's "brand" in regard to what is and isn't appropriate for the product. Art directors are also responsible for coordinating with the other disciplines within the game pipeline such as game developers, designers, and project managers. In the end, any piece of art for a project—be it an in-game asset or marketing materials—is ultimately his or her responsibility.

Cross-Pollination

As we've mentioned throughout this text, game development is where art and technology meet. As a result, the synergy between multiple disciplines is vital in ensuring a strong product. No discipline works in a bubble, be it art, design, engineering, or product management. *Communication is vital* between these diverse groups. As an artist, the success of the work and the game depends on your ability to communicate and relate to these other disciplines. Taking time to examine and understand what it is the different groups do and what challenges they face will only serve to strengthen your overall contribution to the game team. You may find that you learn just as much about making games from the "non-art" groups as you do from fellow game artists. The dialogue and cross-pollination of skills can often be the most efficient and rewarding aspect of game creation. With this in mind, let's take a look at some of the other disciplines that make up a typical game production team.

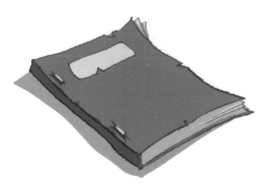

Game Designer

A game designer's role is one that is incredibly complex and that, when boiled down, equates to making the gameplay immersive while creating the best product possible for the target demographic. We mentioned previously that with film production, the genesis for a project typically takes the form of a *script*, and in games, the equivalent is a *design document*, which lays out the entirety of the gameplay in written form. The design document describes the characters, world, features, quests, and so on. It is also the responsibility of the game design team to ensure that elements of the game such as difficulty of gameplay and economy are balanced properly. As with the art team and depending on the size of the game, budget, and so on, this role is often fragmented into multiple roles:

Lead designer—The lead designer is typically in charge of the primary vision of the project and often works closely with the art director on establishing the look of the game by communicating the settings, narrative, characters, demographics, and so on.

Level designer—The level designer develops the gameplay for specific individual levels, features, missions, and so on. The person in this role lays out the challenges and skills entirely based on the story's concept and is primarily responsible for gameplay.

Economy designer—An economy designer's responsibility is that of understanding how the game works as a service and how the customers behave within it. This often involves coordinating with the analytics teams to identify and develop monetization drivers and tuning the game's economy via virtual products and currency.

Game Developer

A game developer is the technician (although his or her work is often as much art as it is science) responsible for merging design and art into an immersive interactive experience through the writing of game code. As a game artist, working closely with a developer is incredibly efficient, as he or she can guide the artist in terms of the art aspects that will work best with the technical constraints of the game engine. Working closely with the development team can lead to less iteration on your part as an artist by avoiding common pitfalls such as performance-draining elements within your art (e.g., vector gradients and complex filters).

Product Manager

In his book *Inspired*, Marty Cagan describes the job of the product manager as someone who "discover[s] a product that is valuable, usable, and feasible." Simply put, product management is the intersection between business, technology, and user experience (art). An effective PM (product manager) is typically well versed in at least one of these areas and passionate about all three. Like all of our previously discussed disciplines, there can be a fragmenting of roles for PMs:

- Revenue PM

- Retention PM (keeping the players coming back)

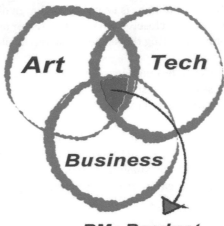

PM: Product Managment

Producer

A producer's role ultimately is coordinating the previous disciplines into a well-organized unit by encouraging communication, maintaining a production schedule, and ensuring both the company's and game team's goals/mission are aligned and being met. This role is often fragmented by the preceding disciplines (e.g., art producer, design producer).

Studio Environment

A game studio environment is meant to be a relaxed space that typically is littered with all manner of toys, games, comics, and so on. Work spaces can vary from studio to studio, though "open floor plans" are very common, as they encourage collaboration and face-to-face dialogue (as opposed to Skype, e-mail, etc.).

It's important to note that due to the nature of game development, there are inevitable "crunch" periods when the studio will work less than ideal hours (6 to 7 days a week and 10 to 14 hours a day in some extreme cases). However, these crunch times generally occur closer to a specific milestone such as a launch date or beta test.

Quick "pivots" in direction from art to design to code are also inevitable. It's production's role (with the aid of the other disciplines) to maintain a sustainable schedule and plan, buffer, and navigate unexpected pivots/crunch periods in a manner that is least likely to cause burnout within the team, as this will inevitably result in a drop in productivity. That being said, in manageable doses, intense deadlines can often produce great work, as they can strip away second-guessing and procrastination that may otherwise slow production down.

ASSIGNMENT 11.1   COMPLETED BIG-BUILDABLE PROP ASSET (5–6) HOURS

Tools

Adobe Photoshop

Description

For this chapter's assignment, we'll be using the color concepts completed in Assignment 9.1 to complete the final big buildable art asset. At this stage, you'll be using the rendering and refinement skills developed in Chapter 10 to complete this complex multistate asset. It's important that you utilize the same process and approach to

- Directional light (global light source)
- Light quality (hard vs. soft)
- Simplified detail
- Photoshop brushes (one or two rendering brushes)
- Shadow/light colors (blend modes)

in order to keep the visual style consistent with your completed small prop assets. In addition, keep in mind that the big buildable is of higher importance within the overall visual hierarchy than your smaller props (harvestables/destructibles) are, so adjust the contrast of value and color accordingly.

(Continued)

ASSIGNMENT 11.1 (CONTINUED)   COMPLETED BIG-BUILDABLE PROP ASSET (5–6) HOURS

Examples

Alexandra DePasse "Completed Big-Buildable"

Florencia Kristiani "Completed Big-Buildable"

(Continued)

ASSIGNMENT 11.1 (CONTINUED)   COMPLETED BIG-BUILDABLE PROP ASSET (5–6) HOURS

Anna Parmentier "FarmVille 2 Club House." (From Zynga, copyright 2009–2017. With permission.)

Purpose

Complete a game-ready three stage "big buildable" asset.

Conclusion

In this chapter, we took a closer look at the various art roles within a 2D game pipeline art team and the disciplines that the art team collaborates with in a game development pipeline. In addition, we completed our large prop asset, "the big buildable," using the basic rendering concepts introduced in Chapter 10.

Quiz

11.1   It is the role of the game developer to merge design and art into an interactive experience. T/F

11.2   Once a mobile/web game goes live, the job of the concept artist is typically done. T/F

11.3   Any piece of art for a project is ultimately the art director's responsibility. T/F

11.4   A production artist's job is that of being the first artist to execute designs for character, creatures, and environments. T/F

Chapter 12

3D Production Pipeline and Marketing Art

CHAPTER OBJECTIVES

In this chapter, we'll explore the various roles for a visual development artist within a 3D game pipeline (*concept artist* and *texture artist*) as well as the 3D-specific roles (*character artist, environment artist, character animator,* and *FX animator*) and their tools (*Maya, Zbrush,* etc.). We'll also define a *marketing artist's* role within a game production pipeline as well examine various types of marketing imagery. Finally, we'll wrap up the isometric game board by completing our final "background game board" asset.

KEY LEARNING OUTCOMES

- Understand the various roles within a 3D production pipeline.
- Explore a marketing artist's role within a game production pipeline.
- Complete final art for the "background game board" asset.

ASSIGNMENT

- Assignment 12.1: Final art: Background Game board (5–6) hours

3D Art Pipeline

In Chapter 9, we examined the visual development artist's role within a traditional 2D game development pipeline while also taking note that 3D graphics are being utilized at an exponential rate in the mobile/web industry. Within a 3D production pipeline,

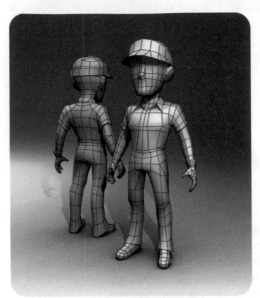

Ryan Murray "FarmVille 2." (From Zynga, copyright 2009–2017. With permission.)

the key players/roles remain essentially unchanged from that of 2D production: Producers, developers, artists, and designers are all represented.

Let's first examine the key players within a 3D production art team.

Character Artist

A *character artist* is responsible for, with the aid of conceptual art, using 3D software packages such as 3D Studio Max and/or Maya to construct 3D models for all character and creature assets within a game. Due to the complexity and importance of characters within gameplay, this role is typically reserved for the experienced/senior 3D artist.

Mark Henriksen "Low Poly Assets" (Blowfish Studios)

Environment Artist

The *environment artist's* responsibilities involve utilizing the same tools as the *character artist* (3D Studio Max and/or Maya) to model all 3D objects seen within the game (with the exception of characters), including vehicles, props, and large structures. Environment artists typically receive concept art for assets that are unique or have specific gameplay elements assigned to them, whereas generic objects such as rocks and computers can often be created with limited concept art or reference images only.

Character Animator

A *character animator* is tasked with bringing the character to life by rigging (a system of "bones" that allow for animation) and animating the previously modeled 3D geometry. A character animator utilizes a variety of 3D tools, including hand animation guided by basic 2D animation principles and procedural animation tools to simulate secondary animations when necessary (e.g., a cape billowing).

"FarmVille 2." (From Zynga, copyright 2009–2017. With permission.)

FX Animator

An *FX animator* is responsible for the creation of any "special" effects within a game (e.g., blood splatter, enchanted fire, coins bursting into confetti). With increasing processing power allowing for more robust and complex particle systems (a technique that simulates difficult to animate phenomena such as *water, smoke,* and *explosions*), FX animation needs have ballooned to demand a dedicated FX artist in many cases.

Note: The following two roles are those that play to the strengths of a visual development artist where their painting and design skills are immediately applicable.

Concept Artist

Concept artist is the ideal role for a visual development artist to inhabit within a 3D art pipeline. This role is essentially identical to that concept artists undertake in a 2D art pipeline in that they're "the first artist to execute the character, creatures, environment, and objects for the world the game design team has mapped out." However, in the 3D design environment, priorities may shift, and there may be an increased emphasis on certain aspects, including:

- Volumetric modeling of characters and objects via advanced rendering techniques (e.g., ambient occlusion), complex lighting, and turnarounds

Tony Trujillo "FarmVille 2." (From Zynga, copyright 2009–2017. With permission.)

- Materials (metal, plastic, etc.) and texture (fur, cloth, etc.) callouts (notice the photo reference of various barns)

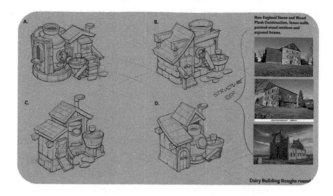

As with most game development roles, depending on the size of production, subdivisions may be made by either skill level or asset type (*junior concept, senior concept, character concept, environment, etc.*).

It's important to note that when in the role of a concept artist (in a 2D or 3D pipeline), an essential question to continually ask yourself is "What is the pertinent information necessary for 'downstream' to complete his or her task?" A modeler requires concepts that clearly emphasize the form/volume of the character/object from multiple angles. These can take the form of turnaround/orthographic renderings, as these provide a modeler with an accurate sense of how a design exits in 3D space.

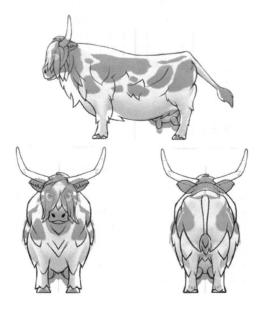

Texture Artist

The application of color, depth, and detail to a 3D object is handled by the *texture artist*. This process includes the painting of a flat 2D image that is then "wrapped" around the model. Ideally, many of the smaller details (individual hairs, metal rivets, buttons, and other small objects) are handled in the texture map, as it will save precious processing power.

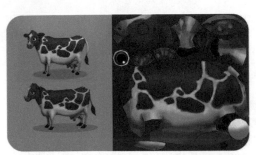

This is an additional role that is well suited for a visual development artist, as it requires translating concept art to polished "in-game" textures and imagery. However, this role, much like the concept art role, benefits tremendously from the artist having a working knowledge of 3D software with an understanding of how the textures are being utilized in the final game asset.

Note: From an organizational standpoint, the previously established art director, senior/lead artist, and so on hierarchy remains in place within a 3D pipeline.

Always keep in mind that depending on which *downstream discipline* you're currently collaborating with, the approach to presentation, detail, color, refinement, pose, and so on should all be guided by the specific needs of that particular discipline. Look to embrace collaboration as communication across disciplines is absolutely crucial at every level of production.

3D for Visual Development

Thus far in this chapter, we've examined various artist roles within a 3D production pipeline, and it should be becoming increasing clear that as a visual development artist working in the games industry, it would behoove you to take an active interest in the workings of 3D modeling, texturing, rigging, and animation. Having, at a minimum, working knowledge of how a particular downstream discipline will be utilizing your work ensures that final assets are efficiently built and also remain true to the initial concept art. Possessing a working knowledge of 3D tools can provide valuable insight into which details will be handled in geometry (modeler) versus painted (texture map) and traps to avoid when designing such details so that they'll translate to a low-poly model.

"What's a *low-poly* model?" you ask. A low-poly model is essentially a 3D model that utilizes a relatively smaller number polygons. They are common in *real-time* applications such as video games (high-poly meshes are utilized more often in 3D animated films and special effects for live action), as the number of polygons has a direct impact on engine performance.

As a result, a low-polygon model framework is highly desirable for game engine performance reasons in the web/mobile games industry and will prioritize simple shapes with minimal, yet readable, detail. For these reasons, hyper-realistically rendered 3D models are prohibitive due to the enormous poly counts that come with them.

In addition to the performance restrictions, there are practical reasons that hyper-realistically rendered mobile games are limited on the market, including that the demographics of the web/mobile industry tend to skew toward "all-ages" as opposed to the teenage/male-centric console games that often leverage hyper-realistic art styles. There's also the simple notion that with the smaller presentation of mobile games, complex details won't be readable on a tablet screen much less a mobile phone.

For these reasons, the "cute" bobble-head proportions shown in the images to the right are optimal (though by no means a rule) for the web/mobile format, as they're low-poly friendly and readable at that smaller mobile smaller scale.

The oversized head, hands, weapons, doorways, and so on place emphasis on important details that are readable at a smaller game scale.

"FarmVille 2 Feeder Asset." (From Zynga, copyright 2009–2017. With permission.)

Brandon Pike "Glumwort Character Concept." (From Zynga, copyright 2009–2017. With permission.)

Brandon Pike "Loading Dock Concept." (From Zynga, copyright 2009–2017. With permission.)

3D Software

Maya and 3D Studio Max—These two dominant 3D software packages have been used since the early days of 3D game development. These off-the-shelf 3D programs allow an artist to model, texture, rig (apply "bones"), and animate while also offering a number of lighting, camera, FX, and rendering engines for cinematics. In the early period of web/mobile games development, 3D Studio Max was more commonly used, as it lent to low poly modeling. However, as 3D game engines such as *Unity* and *Unreal* become more of an option for mobile game development, Maya is being used for 3D needs at an increasing rate.

Zbrush and Mudbox—Both look to mimic a more tactile sculpting feel in a 3D environment that can be appealing to 2D artists who may otherwise be somewhat intimidated by the modeling tools used in the previously mentioned Maya and 3D Studio Max. These programs lend to high-resolution models (the trade-off of using the more tactile modeling tools) and support upward of billions of polygons, which allows for modeling intricate details. Due to the preference of low-poly models in the web/mobile industry, these tools are typically reserved for 3D model concepts and texture painting; however, they can be excellent tools for a 2D artist to experiment with when working with 3D sculpting/modeling.

Google Sketchup—This is a free 3D software package available from Google that has a robust library of easily downloadable models. This is an excellent entry point for artists new to 3D and as tool for a 2D artists, as you can quickly mock up fairly complex perspectives and environment references to inform 2D concepts.

Mobile 3D applications—An increasing number of 3D modeling programs are available for mobile devices (smartphone/tablets), and while they lack the robust toolsets and features of the earlier 3D packages, these tools can be used on the go (iPad/iPhone) to model and texture. As a bonus, many of these tools models can be exported or imported from on-the-go devices to any of the previously mentioned programs.

Tools include:

- Shapr3D

- 123 Sculpt

- Forger

In addition to the roles pointed out as being appropriate for a visual development artist who is part of a 3D art team (concept artist/texture artist), there are roles that fall outside of the game "asset" pipeline that also require the skills of a visual development artist:

- UI (user interface) artist (see Chapter 13)

- Marketing artist

Marketing Art

A marketing artist's role is often tricky to define but can be boiled down to working with *external* art (as opposed to *internal* "in-game" art) that is used to "sell" the product to either project stakeholders within a company (a new game pitch to a CEO, for example) or, more commonly, the buying public. In traditional console gaming, this role would entail art for packaging (box art) and displays, as well as advertising images for popular print and digital news publications. Due to the fluid nature of the industry, the needs and venues for these materials shift and evolve. However, the goal remains the same. Working with a marketing team requires the artist to have a complete understanding of the game's "brand" or core values (what is and is

Duncan Barton "ChefVille." (From Zynga, copyright 2009–2017. With permission.)

Tony Trujillo "FarmVille 2." (From Zynga, copyright 2009–2017. With permission.)

not appropriate for a product). While often embedded within a game's art team, a marketing artist frequently collaborates with a company's marketing/ brand team and acts as the primary link between these groups. The art director of a game project is responsible for every piece of visual imagery for the game, and the marketing brand team is responsible for spreading the message and values of the company as a whole. Working with these two teams to satisfy both priorities, which at times can be at odds with one another, can be the primary challenge of a marketing artist. Establishing a "message" and visual approach is vital prior to beginning work on any marketing art.

A well-organized art team shapes the "in-game" production pipeline around the idea that marketing materials will be needed and will create workflows that lend to in-game assets and concept art being repurposed quickly for marketing purposes. An example of this is the "soft lighting" application in combination with the more refined concept art we examined in Chapter 9.

Achieving these goals is not always easy, as the scale and restrictive game view (side-scroller, isometric, etc.) don't always immediately lend to polished/dynamic marketing artwork.

In-game art:

"Angry Birds 2 Game Screen." (From Rovio, copyright 2009–2017. With permission.)

Marketing art:

"Angry Birds 2 Marketing Image." (From Rovio, copyright 2009–2017. With permission.)

Depending on the marketing needs and budget of a production, a full-time marketing artist may not be feasible. As a result, a member (or multiple members) of the art team will be tasked with generating marketing materials.

Types of Marketing Art

Aspirational Images

Aspirational images can include a wide variety of imagery, including posters, advertisements, and visual target art. Following is a collection of images that run the gamut of in-game loading screens to promotional images. What they have in common is that they are all highly polished from an art standpoint and are not locked to any specific in-game format or style such as the isometric angle of your final projects assets.

"Rubber Tacos." (From Zynga, copyright 2009–2017. With permission.)

The early aspirational image used to sell major stakeholders on the look of "FarmVille 2" (which we examined in Chapter 4) is considered to be an internal marketing image, as it was one of the earliest images created for the project and was meant to act as the initial "visual target" in terms of style and tone.

Tony Trujillo "FarmVille 2 Aspirational Image." (From Zynga, copyright 2009–2017. With permission.)

Logo

Logos are vital to a game product, and their design needs to be approached in the same manner as any of the other various assets of a game by using tools such as shape design, color, and line quality to communicate as

"Rubber Tacos Logo." (From Zynga, copyright 2009–2017. With permission.)

"FarmVille Haunted Hallow Logo." (From Zynga, copyright 2009–2017. With permission.)

much about the theme/setting of the game as possible while also establishing the tone and style. Communicating all of this information can be challenging, as logos are meant to be simple and iconic due to being presented in any number of large and small formats.

The following "Rubber Tacos" logo communicates the fun/playful nature of the game by the rounded soft letters of the font, shiny surfaces, and warm inviting color palette.

In contrast, FarmVille's "Haunted Hallow" expansion logo also conveys a sense of playfulness with the rounded edges of the elements, but this feel is contrasted by the spookier elements such as the dripping effect, bats, and use of black/ cool greens in the color palette.

Note: Take note of how these appear to be completed in the same manner as our character assets with the vector tools. These tools are ideal, as they lend well to keeping the logos simple, clear, and readable for a number of different display scales.

Outside of the previously mentioned assets, there may be additional types of marketing material needs, including:

- *Cross-promotional materials*—Live games occasionally participate in cross-promotional events that can involve a game feature/character/mini-game that utilizes the brand of a celebrity, intellectual property, or product.

- *Social media*—With the rise social media and fan pages/sites, game teams often provide preview images and promotional materials to build excitement for a new game or feature.

- *Merchandise*—Merchandise is a powerful marketing tool not just for additional revenue stream(s) but also for generating exposure and expanding the brand/ mythology of the game. The Finnish game studio Rovio (makers of "Angry Birds") has been able to create an entire universe for the game's characters primarily through merchandising in the form of storybooks, toys, and apparel that culminated with an animated feature film.

ASSIGNMENT 12.1   FINAL ART: BACKGROUND GAME BOARD (5–6) HOURS

Tools

Photoshop CS4 and up

Description

In this assignment, we'll work to wrap up the isometric game board by completing our "background game board" asset. Make sure to emphazise polish and depth/scale via atmospheric perspective.

Alexandra DePasse "Final Background Game Board Asset"

Sunny Yu-Chin Tien "Final Background Game Board Asset"

(Continued)

ASSIGNMENT 12.1 (CONTINUED)   FINAL ART: BACKGROUND GAME BOARD (5–6) HOURS

Take a look at the examples and note how each has managed to effectively "push back" the game board visually with the muted contrast and color temperature to frame the individual assets.

Having your completed character and prop assets available on a separate layer in Photoshop is recommended for quick comparison and balancing of contrast (visual hierarchy). Once balanced, congratulations are in order, as you've now completed the personalized isometric game board project (see in the following).

Alexandra DePasse "Final Isometric Game Board"

Conclusion

In this chapter, we took a closer look at the roles for a visual development artist within a 3D game pipeline (concept artist and texture artist) and 3D-specific roles (character artist, environment artist, character animator, and FX animator) and the associated tools (Maya, Zbrush, etc.). We also identified a marketing artist's role within a game production pipeline and examined a variety of marketing imagery. Finally, we completed the last asset required for our isometric game board, our "background game board" asset.

Quiz

12.1 Concept artist and texture artist are both roles that a visual development artist can occupy in a 3D game production pipeline. T/F

12.2 An art director is responsible for all aspects of an art team's duties. T/F

12.3 High-polygon 3D models typically lend well to web/mobile games. T/F

12.4 Merchandising art does not typically utilize a 2D artist's skills. T/F

12.5 A smart art team will shape an in-game production pipeline around the idea that marketing materials will be needed. T/F

Chapter 13

User Interface and User Experience

CHAPTER OBJECTIVES

In this chapter, we'll continue identifying roles that leverage visual development skills within a web/mobile game pipeline by examining how (*UI*) *user interface* and (*UX*) *user experience* compare and their roles within a digital product. In addition, we will explore supplemental mobile game portfolio materials in the form of basic UI elements and the *side-scroll* game concept.

KEY LEARNING OUTCOMES
- Understand the role of a UI/UX designer.
- Complete three UI assets.
- Complete a refined side-scroll concept.

ASSIGNMENTS
- Assignment 13.1: UI Assets (3–4) hours
- Assignment 13.2: Side-scroll Mini Game Concept (5–6) hours

User Interface and User Experience

Out of the roles we've examined so far in which visual development artists can apply their skill-set (Concept, Production, Marketing, etc.), the last is that of a *user interface* (*UI*) artist. Often combined with the role of the *user experience* (*UX*) artist, *UI* is visual role yet operates as a separate disciple from the art team that we've described up to this point. However, the nature of the work requires continuous interaction with the *art, game design*, and *product teams*. We'll be focusing primarily on the UI portion of the UI/UX role, as it provides the "front-facing" visual aspect of the two.

Before we dive into how our visual development skills can be applied to this discipline, we should first break down what exactly UI and UX design is.

UI Wireframe

"Rockabilly Beatdown" (Rumblecade)

User experience (*UX*) *artist*—User experience involves the emotional response elicited from a human–computer interaction. This can be applied to all types of human–computer interactions, whether it's making a call on your smartphone or navigating the menu on your media player. It includes the ease and efficiency of navigating a product. Apple in particular has long been a proponent of the importance of strong, intuitive UX and as result is known for its products' ease of use. Great UX is why small children are able to navigate devices as complex as tablets.

In the web and mobile games industry, strong UX is vital as game designs have become increasing complex and the ability to clearly communicate to players the *what*, *when*, and *how* of their game interactions will ultimately make or break a product. A UX designer maps out these navigations in the form of "wireframes," which emphasize the flow of a particular gameplay or feature. As we can see by the example to the left, these wireframes can be rough from a visual standpoint but act as a framework by which the UI artist will ultimately design the necessary buttons, icons, and other visual elements that make up the interface.

User interface (*UI*) *artist*—So, what do UI artists do? Well, their role is that of working with a game designer and/or a dedicated user experience designer to create the art a player will use to navigate gameplay. A UI artist essentially populates the wireframes we mentioned above with art assets that communicate function and reinforce the overall style of the project.

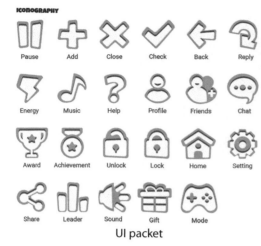

UI packet

"Rockabilly Beatdown" (Rumblecade)

Due to the size restrictions of web/mobile presentation, user interface designers utilize both graphic design and illustration skills to create the visual representation of the user experience. The art must be intuitive and graphically interesting while also not overwhelming the main the game screen (such as our isometric game board). This is a role that depends on logic-based design more so than any other art role we've discussed up to this point and requires extensive communication with multiple disciplines within a game production pipeline, including the aforementioned UX designers, developers, and game designers.

Examples of common UI elements include:

- *Player HUD (heads-up display)*— Health bar, energy meters, experience (player progress), currency, and so on.

- *Buttons*—Call to action (CTA) (e.g., start game), strike, move, and so on.

- *Additional*—Settings, menus, pop-ups, toaster (in game notifications), win congratulatory moments/ animations.

- *Text callouts*—"You're on fire!"

"Hoops Against Friends." (From Zynga, copyright 2009–2017. With permission.)

These are vital components of game design in traditional console games and even more so with web/mobile games. As the mobile/web sector has seen dramatic expansion, the demand for UI/UX in games and applications has expanded along with it. UI will continue to be highly sought after discipline and as a game artist, it's an incredibly marketable skill set to add to your portfolio.

When designing and completing various UI assets, look to keep them simple and graphic as due to the small scale at which they'll be presented, overly detailed/rendered elements will either not read or—worse—distract from the gameplay elements. In addition, look to ensure the UI elements design reinforce the game's style and aesthetic through consistent shape design, material/texture, and color palette.

Leonardo Romano "UI Packet"

Summary

Good UI:

- Is intuitive and easy to use

- Provides ease of information navigation

- Presents a visual design that reinforces the project's style/aesthetic

Bad UI:

- Is overly complicated or has an unclear flow

- Has a generic design (bland non–project-specific art)

- Has sluggish performance (lack of optimized art assets)

Game Portfolio Additions: Side-Scroll Mini Game

As we look to round out our web/mobile game portfolio materials, examples of concepts/ assets utilizing additional common game views (which we discussed all the way back in Chapter 1) can be particularly effective. Up to this point, we've focused primarily on the timeless isometric game view; however, there are multiple other commonly utilized "game views" within the web and mobile game industries that we can leverage for portfolio purposes. "Side-scroll" is one such game view; much like the isometric game view, it's inherently *game-centric* in terms of appearance and has experienced a resurgence in use due in part to the popularity of physics-based games such as the aforementioned "Angry Birds" and its simplicity in design and development.

"Mini Games" have long been a staple of the game industry and almost always utilize a more simplified approach in both appearance and gameplay (e.g., pressing a few buttons at specific intervals) when compared to the main game. Mini Games often take the form of a bonus stage or secret level, or they can be offered separately for free as a promotional tool for the primary game. They're added for varying effects such as to push engagement and expand on the game's world/narrative.

As it relates to the materials we've produced thus far (for our isometric game board), approaching the side-scroll materials for our project as a Mini Games within our primary isometric game board will offer the chance to translate our existing isometric designs to an even simpler style presentation (to complement that simple minigame gameplay) while expanding the project's world by showcasing a fresh location. This also provides opportunities for artists to push additional variety in their portfolio materials.

As we can see with the above example, the visual design priorities we've been utilizing throughout the creation of our isometric game board are on display in the side-scroll as well in that the emphasis should be on:

Leonardo Romano "Side-Scroll Mini Game Concept"

- Establishing depth via overlap, diminution, and atmospheric perspective

- Reinforcing strong visual hierarchy by controlling temperature, color, and saturation

- Ensuring consistent global lighting

- Optimizing figure proportions and design for the web and mobile scale

- Providing clear and intuitive UI elements

Hyoni Yim "Side-Scroll Thumbnail"

The development and design process for a side-scrolling game is the same as for isometric asset designs in that we begin with a simple, yet readable, sketch.

After which we'll explore color and lighting combinations that best fit the setting/mood the environment should convey via color concepts. (*Note:* For the sake of variety, look to develop color/lighting arrangements that contrast with the main isometric game board.)

Color Concepts

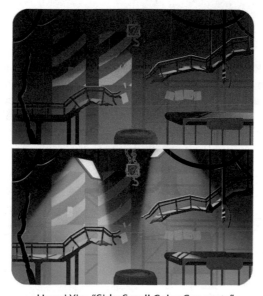

Hyoni Yim "Side-Scroll Color Concepts"

Once you have settled on a color concept, you can move forward with breaking down the various elements (characters, props, UI) and refining/completing the individual assets.

Proceed to the Refinement of Individual Assets

Make it a priority to keep individual assets as simple and graphic as possible to ensure they both read at the already reduced scale and communicate that simplicity of game play. A graphic/shape–based design sensibility can be more effective than a rendered painterly approach for minigames and will infuse stylistic variety in the overall project materials. The vector tools we utilized for our character assets are particularly useful (though by no means required) when completing these assets.

Hyoni Yim "Final Side-Scroll Concept"

Keep in mind that the final environment asset should be treated as three separate layers in the form of foreground, middle ground, and background layers. This will ensure depth and enable the development team to implement a *parallax scroll* (which employs multiple scrolling layers to create the illusion of depth and a psuedo-3D effect in an otherwise 2D scrolling game).

Foreground, Middle Ground, and Background

This will also provide us with an opportunity to showcase UI design in the form of assets mentioned previously in the chapter such as health meter, play, attack, and sound.

ASSIGNMENT 13.1 UI ASSETS (3-4) HOURS

Tools

Adobe Photoshop CS4 and up

Description

In this assignment, you'll complete four commonly used UI elements for your project.

- Health meter

- XP/energy

- Play button

- Collectable (coin, gem, fuel, etc.)

(Continued)

ASSIGNMENT 13.1 (CONTINUED)   UI ASSETS (3-4) HOURS

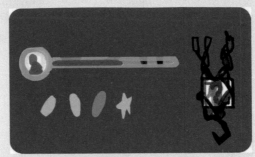

UI Asset Sketch

Completed UI

ASSIGNMENT 13.2   SIDE-SCROLL MINI GAME CONCEPT (5–6) HOURS

Tools

Adobe Photoshop CS4 and up

Description

In this assignment, you'll complete a refined side-scroll game view of your project based around the "Mini Game" concept for the purpose of rounding out your web/mobile game portfolio materials.

Completed Sidescroll With UI

Your final refined side-scroll minigame concept should include:

- One *character* asset
- Two *prop* assets (obstacle/opponents)
- One *environment* asset consisting of three layers (foreground, middle ground, and background)

Conclusion

In this chapter, we continued to identify roles that leverage visual development skills within a game pipeline by examining how *user interface* and *user experience* compare as well as their roles within development of a digital product. In addition, we explored supplemental mobile game portfolio materials in the form of basic UI elements and the *sidescroll* game view. Finally, we completed a side-scroll concept that included three basic UI elements.

Quiz

13.1 User interface is an effective tool for navigation. T/F

13.2 Games are presented at a smaller scale on a mobile device. T/F

13.3 A "main title screen" typically does not include UI/UX elements. T/F

13.4 UI is the goal, UX is the tool. T/F

13.5 Side-scroll is a game-specific composition. T/F

Chapter 14

Portfolio Tips and Parting Words

CHAPTER OBJECTIVES

In this final chapter, we'll wrap up the core concepts explored throughout this book and discuss how visual development artists can best present their work in a portfolio setting. This will include examining the advantages of a physical versus digital portfolio and the utilization of social media to expand your audience and personal brand. We will also review best practices for portfolio preparation and interview etiquette. Finally, we'll discuss the compilation of an 11-page portfolio consisting of the materials completed in the assignment up to this point.

KEY LEARNING OUTCOMES
- Understand the priorities of a visual development portfolio.
- Compile an 11-page web/mobile visual development portfolio.

ASSIGNMENT
- Assignment 14.1: Completed Portfolio (3–4) hours

State of the Industry

As should by now be apparent, the web/mobile game industry continues to grow and evolve. We mentioned previously (see Chapter 12) that with the increased push toward higher-end 3D graphics and complex game designs, anticipating and preparing for these and other

trends is your responsibility as a visual development artist. Keep in mind, however, that despite this push toward 3D, many games currently pursue a 2D production pipeline. Though as tools such as *Unity* and *Unreal Engine* become the standard, the lines between a 2D and 3D production are quickly becoming indistinguishable. With the industry's transition from web-based games such as those found on the Facebook platform to mobile devices (tablet, smart-phone) native to the IOS and Android

platforms (though the web ecosystem, particularly on Facebook, is still very healthy), a key takeaway from this book should be that with your ability to master the basic fundamentals of visual design in addition to diligently keeping up to date on industry trends (such as virtual/augmented reality) in art and technology, you will be in an excellent position to carve out a path in the gaming industry. When navigating employment opportunities, keep in mind that game companies are incredibly varied in terms of products and strategies and as a result, your portfolio's materials should reflect this.

Portfolio Priorities

Artists' portfolios are their most effective tools when seeking employment in the games industry and whether in a physical (bound case, printed book, etc.) or digital (personal website, social media account, etc.) format, there are a few things to keep in mind:

- *What is your message and who is your target audience*? Make sure that the materials that make up the bulk of your portfolio are representative of the current industry, project, genre, and so on that you're targeting.

- *Keep it simple.* Less work is ok as long as it's of high quality and relates to the position/role. In general, 10–15 portfolio pages is more than adequate.

- *Present a variety of materials.* Make sure that your portfolio includes a number of different asset types (*environments, props, characters,* etc.) and style explorations (e.g., concepts to be used in the creation of 3D models and designs such as vector that inform 2D art pipelines). Also, be sure to include development materials such as sketches, studies, and thumbnails, as potential employers need to see how an artist problem-solves, explores, and iterates before settling on a final design.

- *Customize your portfolio.* When applying to a specific project or company, make sure to organize your portfolio in a way that best lines up with that company or client's products. For instance, if an artist were to interview at a company that specialized in children's education applications, he or she should do his or her best with the materials he or she has to front-load their portfolio with examples that best line up with that company's products. A portfolio full of art that is tonally/stylistically different than the products typically done by the team interviewing an artist can give the impression that the artist would rather be making other types of games.

- *Include only your absolute best work.* If there's any piece within your portfolio that you feel the urge to preface with "Well, this isn't my best work" or "I usually do better," then remove it immediately. An art director can evaluate a candidate's skill level within the first few pages of a portfolio.

- *Provide supplemental material.* Toward the back of your portfolio, it's a good idea to dedicate a few pages to work such as life drawings, traditional media paintings, illustrations, or any other pieces that don't fall specifically into the "game art" or "visual development" categories yet show additional versatility and/or personal interests.

Page Layout

The following template shows a fairly standard approach to presenting your work in that the goal is to spotlight the process through sketches and development art along with the final design/asset. Look to tell a story with the way in which you've organized the materials on the portfolio page.

A landscape aspect ratio is recommended, and adding simple design elements to the portfolio page layouts can be effective as long as they do not overpower the images that they're framing.

Brandon Pike "CastleVille Portfolio Page." (From Zynga, copyright 2009–2017. With permission.)

Portfolio Formats

Traditional

There are a number of different formats to consider when presenting work to a potential client. While having a digital/online presence is crucial, assembling a traditional portfolio is just as important.

Classic Portfolio Case

This is an approach that involves high-quality color prints arranged within a portfolio binder/case. Prices vary depending on the quality of the portfolio binder (as well as the individual portfolio page prints); however, these provide the advantage of being more flexible in that an artist can continuously arrange and rearrange work to fit the needs of the viewer (art director, recruiter, etc.) or specific project.

Custom Printed Book

Another approach involves publishing a personalized booklet by uploading a digital portfolio (PDF file) to print-to-order sites such as:

- Lulu.com

- Blurb.com

Both options are effective; however, a printed booklet can act as both a portfolio and a marketing tool in that with the printing of multiple copies, they can be mailed, handed out, or sold/distributed to a wider audience via venues such as trade shows and online retailers.

Keep in mind that your goal is to stand out from the pack not just in terms of content but also presentation. Doing whatever you can to personalize your presentation, be it hand-making and binding your own book or using a creative template to frame your work will set yours apart from the other hundreds of visual development portfolios.

Digital

With the rapid advancement of technology, opportunities to get your work in front of recruiters, art directors, and a general audience have multiplied exponentially. Art directors/recruiters often accept digital portfolios consisting of JPG images or a complied version in a PDF.

However, keep in mind that many are wary of downloading attachments due to the risk of viruses and the hassle of managing large files. The most common and effective strategy for a digital portfolio is to approach it from three fronts.

Personal Website

A personal website is still the most effective digital portfolio. This should be solely dedicated to your visual development work (no photos of cats) and reflect your skillset and your "brand." Organize your work in a simple, easy to navigate layout.

Sites such as *Squarespace* and *Wix* offer a variety of easy to populate templates for you to build and customize your own personal site with.

- Squarespace.com

- Wix.com

Here, to the right, is an example of an effective visual development artist's site.

Tony Trujillo "Personal Website"

Online Communities

Artists can also take advantage of a variety of online art communities for their personal portfolios, including:

- *ArtStation*—https://www.artstation.com

- *Behance*—https://www.behance.net

- *DeviantArt*—http://www.deviantart.com/

- *CGSociety*—http://www.cgsociety.org/

- *ConceptArt*—http://www.conceptart.org

These art communities have a very strong aspect of self-promotion. Which, while we're on the topic of self-promotion ...

Social Media Platforms

The rise of social media platforms such as Twitter, Facebook, and Instagram have allowed for instant access to artists and have become a powerful tool for self-promotion and marketing. Keep in mind that while these will not necessarily operate as your main online portfolio site, they can work to build your audience by showcasing process sketches and more "snack-bite-sized" art postings.

As an artist, you should always be on the lookout for new tools that allow you to connect with an audience and bring exposure to your personal "brand"—the ones discussed in this chapter are but a snapshot of what is currently available.

Interview Etiquette

So let's say that you've compiled your portfolio, applied to a game studio's job posting, and have been called in for an onsite interview. What are some things to keep in mind when going into the interview process?

First, it's crucial that you familiarize yourself with the current state of the industry by researching relevant companies, trends, and technologies prior to applying for the job. There is no excuse for not having familiarized yourself with a particular company's games and brand prior to an interview. What type of products is the company known for? What style or design language unifies their projects? What are the target demographics? These are important questions to ask yourself prior to interviewing, as they will more than likely come up in one form or another in the interview.

Once these questions have been answered (and as previously mentioned, you have customized your portfolio presentation to the potential employer), make sure to:

- *Dress the part.* Something as simple as your appearance communicates a lot about your interest in a role and your organizational skills. To put it bluntly, if an applicant can't organize himself or herself and his or her appearance, how can he or she be expected to be able to operate within a complex work environment that requires collaboration amongst multiple disciplines? Game studios are often casual environments; however, for an interview, make a good first impression. Business casual attire is a requirement.

- *Ask questions.* This may seem obvious, though as a result of nerves or not wanting to come across too eager, candidates often forget to ask questions. Who will be my manager? What types of tools/programs does the art team utilize? Asking questions shows you're engaged and interested.

- *Don't be defensive.* This cannot be stressed enough. When an art director/recruiter/someone else is reviewing your work, no matter how off base you think their opinion is, listen and answer any questions they may have.

ASSIGNMENT 14.1   COMPLETED PORTFOLIO (3–4) HOURS

Tools

Adobe Photoshop

Description

With this final assignment, you'll be compiling all work (including concepts and final assets) completed up to this point into a comprehensive 11-page portfolio consisting of the following items.

Characters

- One page for sketches/color concepts

- One page for final character assets

Big Buildable

- One page for sketches/color concepts

- One page for final three-stage big buildable asset

Props

- One page for sketches/color concepts

- One page for final assets

Background Game Board

- One page for color concepts/completed background game board

- One page for final completed isometric game board + all the previous assets

User Interface Elements

- One page for color concepts/completed UI assets

(Continued)

ASSIGNMENT 14.1 (CONTINUED)   COMPLETED PORTFOLIO (3-4) HOURS

Side-Scroll

- One page for sketches/color concepts

- One page for final side-scroll concept with UI elements

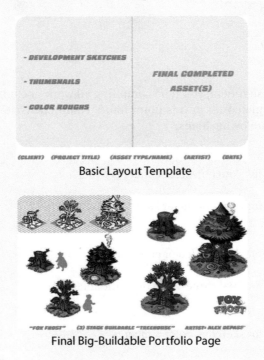

Basic Layout Template

Final Big-Buildable Portfolio Page

Conclusion

In this final chapter, we reviewed several core concepts explored throughout this book and discussed how visual development artists can best present their work in a portfolio setting. We examined the advantages of a physical versus digital portfolio and utilizing social media to expand an artist's audience and personal brand. We also reviewed best practices for portfolio preparation and interview etiquette. Finally, we'll compile an 11-page portfolio consisting of the materials completed in the assignments up to this point.

Parting Words

As we are at the end of this book, I'd like to congratulate you on completing it. Hopefully you've found the concepts and materials we've discussed enlightening, entertaining, and informative as we explored the fundamentals of design and visual development while also exposing you to opportunities available in an ever-evolving web/mobile gaming industry. This is an exciting time in games, as the traditional console industry has been disrupted by the exploding market around web and mobile games. While this disruption may scare/frustrate some of the more entrenched traditional gamemakers, this has created countless opportunities and opened up a whole sector of games, players, and platforms that previously did not exist. One thing is clear, though, everyone—no matter their age or demographic—*loves* playing games and if anything, this disruption has proved this. The ability to communicate to an audience via the tools and concepts we've covered will go a long way toward identifying and generating opportunities for artists within the web/mobile game and entertainment industry as a whole. This author wishes you the best of luck with your continued growth. I'll leave you with a few bits of wisdom from the legendary designer Alex Toth[*]:

> *"Eliminate the superfluous, the unnecessary. Be lazy!"*
> *"Edit your art continuously, at every stage. Save work!"*
> *"Focus on the remaining (important) picture elements."*
> *"Emphasize what IS important in a scene. Save drawing!"*
> *"Authenticate devices, objects, machines, locales, furniture, etc.... to lend credibility!"*
> *"Be honest to it. Give it all you've got! Enhance it!"*
> *"Analyze everything you see—be critical. Positively so!"*
> *"See—observe—remember! Build up your memory file!"*
> *"Spend more time THINKING—about WHAT and what NOT to draw, and HOW—and you'll do LESS DRAWING!"*

Best of luck!
—Chris

Quiz

14.1 Despite a push toward 3D, there are still many games that pursue a 2D production pipeline. T/F

14.2 It's important to never be defensive during a portfolio review. T/F

14.3 Asking questions as a candidate is important during an interview. T/F

14.4 Personal artists' websites are not effective venues for a digital portfolio. T/F

14.5 Social media tools such as Twitter, Facebook, and Instagram are powerful tools for self-promotion and marketing. T/F

---

[*] Toth, A. and Hitchcock, J. *DEAR JOHN: The Alex Toth Doodle Book*, 2006. Octopus Press, Portland, OR.

Answer Key

1.1	True
1.2	True
1.3	False
1.4	False
1.5	True
2.1	True
2.2	True
2.3	False
2.4	False
3.1	False
3.2	True
3.3	True
4.1	True
4.2	False
4.3	True
4.4	False
5.1	True
5.2	True
5.3	False
5.4	True
6.1	True
6.2	False
6.3	True
6.4	False
7.1	False
7.2	True
7.3	True
7.4	True
7.5	True
8.1	False
8.2	True
8.3	True
8.4	True
8.5	False
9.1	False
9.2	True
9.3	False
9.4	True
10.1	False

10.2	False
10.3	True
10.4	True
11.1	True
11.2	False
11.3	True
11.4	False
12.1	True
12.2	True
12.3	False
12.4	False
12.5	True
13.1	True
13.2	True
13.3	False
13.4	False
13.5	True
14.1	True
14.2	True
14.3	True
14.4	False
14.5	True

Index